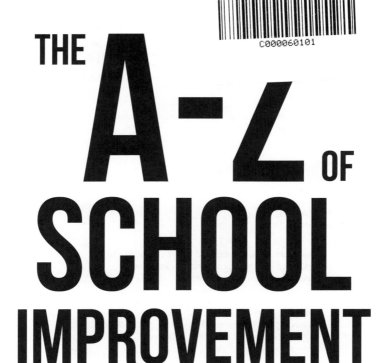

THE A-Z OF SCHOOL IMPROVEMENT

TIM COULSON

SERIES EDITOR: ROY BLATCHFORD

JOHN CATT

FROM HODDER EDUCATION

To order, please visit www.johncatt.com or contact Customer Service at education@hachette.co.uk / +44 (0)1235 827827.

ISBN: 9781036005009

© Tim Coulson 2024

First published in 2024 by
John Catt from Hodder Education,
An Hachette UK Company
15 Riduna Park, Station Road,
Melton, Woodbridge IP12 1QT
www.johncatt.com

Typeset in the UK.

Printed in the UK.

A catalogue record for this title is available from the British Library.

To Alison, without whom nothing would have been possible.

CONTENTS

Section 2

FOREWORD

We are all deeply interested in doing a little better tomorrow what we did today. That is what I have encountered in working with colleagues on school improvement over many years in the education business.

I first met the extremes of 'school failure' full on when, twenty years ago, I moved from secondary headship to join the highly respected school improvement division (SID) within Her Majesty's Inspectorate. For three years I travelled up and down the country monitoring special, primary and secondary schools which for one reason or another had fallen on hard times, some to the point of desperation.

In all these contexts, hard conversations – always with a humble twinkle in the eye – were the norm.

As a monitoring inspector you aimed to make yourself redundant: to help accelerate the school's journey of self-improvement; to share in the school's eventual successes; to see pupils, teachers and leaders regain self-esteem and pride in their place of work. It does not surprise me that I have stayed in personal and professional contact with most of the headteachers who led those improvement journeys for their school communities.

These leaders taught me so much in intense contexts. I salute them.

Do failure and dysfunction happen because of conspiracy, cock-up or benign neglect? Rarely in my experience is failure wilful. It can be through ignorance in the Latin sense of the word *ignoscere* – not knowing. It can often be complex to untangle. It is rare for good schools with well embedded systems to decline badly, though not unknown. Sometimes an extreme event in a local community can damage a school's reputation irretrievably.

It would be fair to say here that the number of 'failing schools' in England has happily been reduced to a minimum, and leaders in those contexts work tirelessly to remedy their shortcomings, ably supported by HMI monitoring visits.

The above commentary has been focused on school improvement from a low starting point. There remain some schools which just bob along, never breaking through to being thriving and confident schools. They survive and falter, rather than flourish. They never quite reach the 'tipping point' which leads to sustaining success. These are hard nuts to crack, often but not always in disadvantaged social arenas.

Then there are the vast majority of schools in neighbourhoods across the country where families are confident in what teachers are providing. In these contexts, leaders are ever restless to improve what they are doing, investing in children and staff alike to ensure the best quality of education, day in and day out.

This is the rich and fascinating spectrum of school improvement. By its very nature, the process of improvement and development is never finished: teachers and leaders *are* deeply interested in doing a little better today what they did yesterday.

****

No matter your context or starting point, this book will speak to you about school improvement, its arts and science, its professional challenges and enormous rewards. No school or school system in the world is better than its teachers and its leaders; and culture trumps systems. This book has that assertion at its core. Its 26 narratives are compelling reading.

In common with all titles in this series, Section One is ordered under the A-Z alphabetical headings. Section Two presents further material for professional development.

Tim Coulson is one of the most highly respected leaders working in English education. He brings to every page a deep knowledge of how schools work in the best interests of their children. To this he adds a unique set of experiences from his work nationally, regionally and locally over the past forty years. A spirit of integrity, inclusion and kindness lies at the heart of this book.

Enjoy his wisdom, practical tips and trenchant analysis: from *Booster* and *Forensic* to *Marginals* and *Resilience*, and twenty-two more!

Roy Blatchford, series editor

SECTION ONE

AMBITION

'Without a vision, the people perish' (*Proverbs*, 29:18). Without ambition there is no school improvement.

In 1997, the new Labour Government introduced 'target setting'. Each school was to set out their ambitions for the results they believed children at different ages might achieve 18 months hence. The then Qualifications and Curriculum Authority was charged with consulting on specific proposals about the detail of what this would involve. Touring and fronting conferences in five major cities were an eye opener – in four venues, constructive dialogue took place about how to make the idea of target setting work practically but in London the balloon went up. Never had such a ridiculous suggestion been proposed and whoever even entertained the idea was simply a Government collaborator. It was symptomatic of an area of the country with both low educational standards and furious objections to being challenged about them.

Yet 25 years later, the capital now leads the way not just in results (and funding) but in its ambitions for its young people. The city has seen remarkable school improvement through that collective ambition. Ambition is contagious. Academy trusts and school leaders across the country are working hard to infect their areas. And now London is having to wake up to other regions having similar ambitions to provide the best for their children.

There may be ambitions in schools about lots of things, but *this* book is about the single-minded drive for school improvement: the ambition that children should experience more, do better, and achieve more. No school leader is without ambition, but many do not fully grasp the sheer extent of the ambition that drives the most successful.

Successful leaders don't just improve schools, they transform them. Everyone wants to lead a good and effective school. Everyone taking over a school in trouble wants it to recover and return respectability to the education it provides to its children. However, some leaders set ambitions that achieve these aims more effectively or quicker. Conversely, school improvement is often limited by leaders' lack of ambition. Rarely do schools achieve their aims better or quicker than the ambitions that their leaders have set.

A school leader sets the weather – if everything is too difficult, the leader should not be surprised if staff are noticeably negative and doubtful of new-fangled ideas achieving much. When leaders are upbeat and positive despite the challenges of the week, it's not surprising to see staff go the extra mile for colleagues and children.

We can all recognise someone with an ambitious mindset. However, unless their ambitions are coherently articulated and spelled out there is a risk that they lead to too many disparate improvement efforts. These may be individually worthy, but together they will not add up to a changed school. Ambition cannot be over-communicated. Tell people what you are going to say, tell people what you want them to hear, and tell people what you have just said. A school leader knows that their communication about their ambition for their school has been effective when she or he hears it told back to them by someone unaware that it was the leader's idea in the first place.

We became teachers to change the world. We know that education provides opportunities and at its best can level the world's unfair playing field. Too much of school performance correlates with their social mix and the prior attainment of its children. Our job is to break the glass ceiling of what we believe is possible – if we don't aspire to this, it undoubtedly won't happen. We want to change the world for those children whose destiny otherwise feels defined by limits on what they can achieve, limits on what they can dream.

Scandals persist – social and racial inequality exists and cannot simply be wished away. A young black girl can be encouraged by teachers to do whatever she wants, whether it is to be a professional in some regard or even an astronaut. However, in reality the chance of her becoming a headteacher is many times less likely than her white friend even if she is much brighter and more suited. With the ambition for social justice comes the dream of change. Without the ambition for social justice the status quo remains by default.

School improvement takes commitment. Even once leaders have established belief through setting a shared ambition, and begin to see progress, a common difficulty is losing sight of the benchmark to which the school is aspiring. It is a big job to put a school back together after a poor period, perhaps following a bad inspection report. Committed leaders can will the school to improve, work unreasonable hours, and build a new school team who will be amazing for the future of the school and still be judged harshly by external evaluation. A disappointing judgement does not negate the progress made but should remind school leaders of the long journey needed for a school to be fully rehabilitated.

Cold, hard, ambition requires a clear understanding of the current barriers to children achieving. This is why the serious school leader needs to be both the helicopter pilot and down in the weeds – keeping an eye on both the overview and the fine detail. For example, most schools wanting to improve should address the climate for learning across the whole school and evaluate progress achieved through the attainment levels that pupils reach. A less precise diagnosis of issues could lead to a myopic focus on smaller contributing factors such as 'weak teachers', or corridor behaviour, without considering the wider picture. The accuracy with which issues are identified will affect the precision of the tactics school leaders choose to employ.

Leaders need a clear 'helicopter pilot' view of the whole picture to step away from specific frustrations – such as 'behaviour not being good enough' – to set the standards across all of the school. However, they also need to be 'down in the weeds' to remember how hard it can be to achieve change, and the support required to help staff right across a school achieve the consistency of language and standards that leaders so desire.

How long does change take? Move a school leader who has had success in improving one school to another needing similar attention and it doesn't take long for the hard reality to dawn that improvement journeys in different schools diverge and success takes varied amounts of time.

Since the start of sponsored academies, there has been an expectation of eight terms before improvement should be subject to inspection. Eight terms, or three school years, across which a new head can make improvements. This timescale feels very different if those responsible first have to determine the effectiveness of an existing head, agree a change is needed, effect that change, and finally recruit a new head (who will now start with considerably less than eight terms to produce results).

Ambition is tempered by the art of the possible. A challenge for leaders is living in the real world of resources, capacity, circumstances, and day-to-day life ... yet being also the constant voice that keeps our ambitions to the fore and sustains the energy to keep focussing on what needs to improve further. Most leaders need help to maintain this determination and not to join those staff who say their school is unique and that outsiders don't understand why strategies that work elsewhere won't work here. Some school leaders will keep an ambition alive through the external support of a coach, taking time to get out and see how the most successful schools do things, or inviting in colleagues they respect to give blunt feedback on where their ambition may be dimming.

Ambitions are never fully achieved (unless they are easy). Consider a school with a great climate, skilled and knowledgeable staff, sensitive and determined leaders, and students who achieve better than ever before. You will still be able to hunt out the least happy children who have few friends, those making least successful progress in their work, and those least successful in conforming to their teachers demands. Is it the job of these children to get better at dealing with their difficulties, or is the school leader's job to ensure that they can overcome these barriers to their own success?

ASIDE

Ambitions for children with SEN

A school should have the ambition that children with special educational needs flourish and do well. This will include meeting the expectations of their Education, Health and Care Plan and achieving academically as well as possible.

Other key measures for children with special educational needs include:

- Participation in the school football team, or any other given area of school life they have selected.
- Participation in extra-curricular activities.
- Most importantly, whether they have friends.

BOOSTER

The start of a school improvement journey is exciting, nerve wracking, and unpredictable. One of the challenges for any school leader on such a journey for the first time is making a difference quickly and yet sustainably. Amongst the big milestones in school improvement journeys are summer results; in particular, the results of 11- and 16-year-olds, how these compare with the national picture, and the extent to which they show improvement on previous years.

Improving results quickly requires close attention to the oldest year group in the school (Year 6 in primary and Year 11 in secondary schools). Giving a lot of attention to these year groups can feel disturbing – even if results improve and this is not only great for the young people themselves but gives a shot in the arm for confidence in the wider improvements that school leaders are looking to achieve. The anxiety is because at the end of this school year this group of children leave the school, and it can feel that the energy that went into them has been lost and is therefore not contributing to the sustainable improvements that are the real goal. However, this concern is misguided. These children have spent their school careers being provided with substandard education and deserve the very best the school can give. You cannot simply write them off.

A key aspect of planned short-term improvements must include making up for lost learning opportunities for those children who have been given substandard education. This approach is often characterised by 'booster' classes (particularly in primary schools). In general, this refers to providing extra lessons in English and maths to children approaching major national assessments or public examinations. In primary schools these classes may be before school, during school breaks, or after school.

In secondary schools they will generally be additional revision classes after school.

A more controversial approach is altering the amount of curriculum space allocated to English and maths so that they take up time that ordinarily would be allocated to other subjects, or even dropping an entire GCSE subject in the months leading up to exams. The current Ofsted framework pressures schools not to adopt such strategies. However, the influence of Ofsted in this area is debatable. Of course, every child should be entitled to the full breath of the curriculum and enjoy every aspect of what schools should provide. However, without skills in reading, writing, and mathematics, children's access to a wider curriculum is severely limited and talk of entitlement is a mirage without the necessary focus on basic skills.

Beyond additional classes, other strategies that can be included in a 'booster' approach are homework packs or revision books that can be used by children and their parents on an ongoing basis during the term or with intensity during school holiday periods. Some schools have found it particularly impactful to provide one-to-one support from the most senior members of staff in the school to either every child, or children within a targeted group. This support could be academic, such as short bursts of coaching in specific areas of work a child finds difficult, or might be organisational and motivational.

In deciding on a particular approach, the key decision is which staff to involve. There is an argument that the teacher doing the day-to-day and timetabled work is best positioned to use any additional time to build on what had already been planned for the children. If teachers' work is sufficient to help children achieve the results the school believes they should achieve, then all is well and good. If, however, what is needed is additional motivation then the booster effort is probably best provided by a different member of staff. In some schools the senior leadership team take this on themselves. At best because they want to set the example of extra discretionary effort, at worst because they can't persuade their wider colleagues to give this effort.

As schools returned to some kind of normality after the covid lockdowns of 2020-21, they were provided with additional funding to support children in catching up on the learning they had lost. Controversially, the government decided to follow the clear research evidence that small group tutoring has the potential to make a significant difference to children's progress. For many years there have been parents who have paid for tutoring for their children outside school – where they have the means to do so. Government funding aimed to make this opportunity available for all children who had fallen behind.

Where schools took this new opportunity seriously, they learned that small group tutoring poses different pedagogic challenges to what teachers of large classes are used to. Interestingly, parents have been quicker to see the power of tutoring than many teachers or senior leaders have been. Such was the unwillingness of some schools to embrace this approach, that there was enough of an underspend that it allowed the government to fund a teacher pay rise to bring an end to national strike action in 2023. This despite this funding being offered in a period when schools were complaining loudly about funding constraints.

Another way of providing additional teaching time for children before they come up to national assessments or public examinations is to use school holiday periods, particularly the Easter holiday shortly prior to tests and exams. Many schools are now open for much of the Easter holiday with additional classes interspersed with food and fun to attract children in. Much less consistent is the extent to which this is simply an expectation placed upon committed staff or an opportunity from which staff receive additional payment. Given the normalisation of such events during Easter, schools and trusts should now be including funding for these events as part of their annual budgets.

A slightly different version of school holiday additional learning is the summer transition weeks that have successfully been held by many secondary schools for new children due to start in September. At their most successful, schools are attracting high percentages of children coming into Year 7 to spend a week at the school in late July or August. At a basic level this helps children find their way around the school, learn familiar faces and experience some of the specialist rooms that will be new to them.

At a more serious level, schools can use this week to set the culture they expect, to identify the strategies that will make a difference – particularly with children it is already clear will find secondary school difficult – and to make sure that children start secondary school building directly on their successes at primary school. It has been the case for many years that secondary teachers are often unaware quite how far children have progressed by the end of Year 6.

As children approach the major milestones at the ends of Year 6 and Year 11, just teaching them more will have some impact. However, a 'booster' approach has a much greater impact when it's not just the teachers who are pushing but the children take over and assume responsibility for being ready for their assessments and examinations. Schools that understand this think carefully about how much extra time is used on English and mathematics and how much is used on strategies for revision, encouraging individual motivation, and individual coaching on areas requested by children.

This chapter started with the dilemma of prioritising short-term gains in results versus long term sustainable score improvement. While my approach here has been a fierce defence of including short-term improvement strategies, no school should be dependent on only these strategies. In some schools this can mean that after a couple of years of 'booster' approaches, these are no longer necessary as the core of a school improvement strategy. The most successful schools focus on all year groups and aim that none reaches their examination years with a mountain to climb. However, even in the most successful schools, with progress being achieved in every year group, these booster strategies are still effective and can add the icing on the cake in terms of results.

ASIDE

Booster lesson checklist

1. Why do some children not attend additional revision classes/ booster classes etc? Do staff know (or assume they do)?
    Understanding causes may help find strategies that overcome whatever barriers to attendance there may be.

2. Are the booster lessons provided just the same as the usual daily lessons?
    They need to cover the same material but engage children differently to help motivate voluntary attendance.

3. When is the best time for booster lessons? Is before school better than after school? or school holiday periods best?
    Why not try them all and see what works?

4. If revision classes are held at the same time for different subjects, how should a child decide which to attend? Or should staff decide for the child?
    Revision class attendance requires motivation so allowing students the choice is likely to help attendance even if it disappoints particular staff.

5. Do children need rewards for attending booster/revision classes?
    Like any incentive or reward in school, the aim is that they become redundant as progress becomes intrinsically rewarding.

CRITICS

School improvement journeys are intense and demanding. They have ups and downs and can be both very rewarding and deeply frustrating. Charting the progress of each school's improvement journey is essential. Having a thoroughly realistic assessment of where that journey has got to – and crucially whether the current strategies are proving successful – helps inform hard-headed decisions on whether to stick with or change the strategies being used.

Good school improvement plans will have plenty of milestones against which to measure progress. Effective governance will monitor these milestones carefully and take stock of the success of the strategies being used.

There will be several people involved in pushing for success in any school improvement journey. As well as the headteacher and the school staff, there will be the school's close supporters. These will include specialists in the key areas where the school needs to improve, whoever it is that is responsible for overseeing the headteacher and, perhaps, other local schools or trusts who are lending their expertise. All of these people are willing the school to succeed. All of these people are determined to exude positivity about the future success of the school. They will all try hard to maintain a clear sight of reality but try as they might all of them will also become heavily invested in the success of the school. It is therefore necessary, from time to time, to commission external critiques of the school's improvements.

External critiques can come in a variety of different forms. Some are about compliance – such as the basic 'Single Central Record' check that all staff recruitment has included the necessary safeguarding checks.

Even these basic audits continue to cause occasional surprises! Wider safeguarding audits include a lot of compliance checks, but really are about the rigour and culture that should be the hallmarks of every school that puts children's safety at the top of its priorities.

In secondary schools, a standard improvement tool has been departmental reviews and assessing the relative strengths across a school. Best practice is to make sure that such reviews address the important interplay between the roles of heads of department, key subject experts, and those experts' line managers. Those line managers will be members of the senior leadership team, and often will not have the same subject knowledge as their team members, but they will still have the responsibility of ensuring a highly effective department.

In many places these reviews have been replaced by the subject 'deep dives' peddled by Ofsted, and which have been at the heart of inspection methodology in the early 2020s. Deep dives now take place in all school inspections, elevating the subject chosen – geography, for example – to the same status as all other subjects, whether the school is an infant school, a grammar school or a special school. At best, deep dives get at what the school is providing for children and how well they are achieving in this specific subject. For less savvy inspectors covering subjects in which they are not experts, though, the credibility of these exercises has been tarnished. Outside the context of inspection, a deep dive can be a useful exercise as long as the reviewer has sufficient subject knowledge to engage with what children have learnt.

In the drive to get to a favourable position before a school is next inspected an external review can be a dry run of the format of that forthcoming inspection.

There are many inspectors who have experience with Ofsted in the education system. However, individuals who continue to inspect for Ofsted are specifically banned from carrying out any kind of review that uses Ofsted's inspection methodology. Schools get around this by making use of recently retired inspectors prepared to bend the rules, as well as individuals who are not inspectors but who have observed enough inspections to be able to carry out something pretty similar. The challenge in this approach is the resources needed to gather and collate all the information that would be collected during an inspection. Organisations that need this level of assurance betray a lack of confidence in their own assessment. In general, a better approach is to use experienced inspectors to focus on the areas which have caused a school the most difficulty; in doing so they will generally pick up any other major concerns that the school should know about.

Three very specific reviews that many academy trusts organise on a regular/annual basis are about behaviour, special educational needs, and safeguarding. Let's look at the first of these. Any review of behaviour needs to go beyond just the most obvious issues in any particular school. Renaming the review to make it clear that it is about the effectiveness of the culture for learning within the school rather than just compliance to the rules is a good basis for a more holistic approach. Within some academy trusts there are not only clearly established expectations for standards of behaviour but set out procedures for implementing routines and ways of working that promote excellent behaviour and a strong culture for learning in every classroom. When academy trusts reach this level of confidence about aligning procedures, reviews are much more straightforward, as are any recommendations that follow.

A personal favourite review is that of provision for children with special educational needs. One approach to this is to have agreed standards in a variety of areas of work and then to use a reviewer to evaluate the extent to which a school meets each of these standards, perhaps using a RAG rating (red/amber/green). While there are many aspects to the successful provision of education for children with all the various special educational needs that may be present in a school, two essential criteria are that SEN children achieve well and have friends.

No matter how strong and rigorous the framework is for each kind of review, its credibility ultimately rests on the reviewer. Credibility is essential to avoid outcomes and recommendations being dismissed as being from someone who does not understand 'the unique circumstances of our school'. Conversely, when organisations such as academy trusts use their own staff to review progress then they need to be alive to the criticism of 'marking their own homework' – that is lacking the perspective to see the school separately from the effort and care poured into improving it.

One approach is to put in place some kind of moderation, for example to have an annual review duplicated by someone from another organisation allowing you to compare the findings of the two reviewers. This is a particularly effective approach with compliance. Another strategy is to build up a relationship with another trust, whereby you mutually share supporting each other in reviews.

A review is only as effective as the follow up that comes next. A sign of how seriously a school leader welcomes scrutiny is the effort put into sharing the findings of reviews. They should at a minimum be shared across senior leadership teams and boards of governors or trustees, but where possible also with all staff and even parents. Furthermore, a review is of little use if it just praises everything. Reviews should lead to action, whether major or merely tinkering. A particularly effective format is when the criteria of progress that are being assessed have been agreed prior to the review. Where possible, reviewers should return to the school – say six weeks later – and comment on the extent of progress and what remains to be done. If concerns continue, then the follow up needs to make it clear that implementing particular recommendations will require greater support.

The word 'review' has been used throughout this chapter, entitled *Critics*. A good critic is a critical friend, willing to give honest but constructive advice. A critical friend will be appreciative and clear about how well or badly a school is implementing the efforts that have gone into its improvement.

ASIDE

School improvement and evaluation in New Zealand

New Zealand's school inspection culture is notably different to England's. Here is what the NZ Education Review Office has to say on the topic of the strategic aims of internal school improvement and external evaluation. Food for thought!

'Twenty-five years of school improvement research has shown that improving schools depends on internal capacity and new learning. It requires motivation (improvement orientation), new knowledge, and the development of new skills, dispositions and relationships. In particular, using indicators to improve practice in schools depends on skill in using data, creating cultures of inquiry, engaging in deep and challenging conversations about practice, and changing long-established beliefs and patterns of practice. Considered this way, indicators and the [evaluation] process itself are tools to support the thinking and action that is part of building professional capital.'

'Periodic external evaluation supports schools in their improvement journeys by providing an independent assessment of their performance in terms of excellence and equity of outcomes for every student, and the extent to which internal conditions support ongoing improvement. Insights gained from an external evaluation can act as a catalyst for change.'

School Evaluation Indicators, Education Review Office, New Zealand.
Available at: https://ero.govt.nz/how-ero-reviews/
schoolskura-english-medium/school-evaluation-indicators.

DFE

At its best the Department for Education (DfE) can be a strong lever for school improvement. Although up until the end of the 1970s the DfE did not see itself as having a role in school improvements, since the 1980s its impact on the school system has been transformational. The William Tyndale affair (1974-75) – sparked by parental protests over radically progressive methods adopted at the William Tyndale Junior School, Islington, and leading to a parliamentary review and the dismissal of several staff – changed everything. Prime Minister James Callaghan made his so-called Ruskin speech about education policy, which now would be seen as fairly mild but then was seen as amazingly radical in terms of government interference in school policy. From the 1980s until the present-day governments have taken the view that they can, and should, affect the school system nationally using the leverage available to them.

Most government ministers have drawn on advice from school leaders they admire. In some cases, this has led to policy development, or even systemic change. In either case a key factor in successful policy shifts is operational leadership within the DfE by school leaders who understand the system and how to affect change. One of the most successful school systems in the world is in Singapore. A striking feature of this system is its strategic use of successful school leaders, dynamically moving them to the schools where they are most needed. The best leaders are also brought into government administration for a period before returning to the school system. This approach allows for cross fertilisation of ideas and expertise.

In England there have been wasted opportunities. The best ministers recognise the importance of providing clarity on their view of what a successful school system looks like and empowering school leaders to implement change. Poorer ministers have allowed themselves to be hemmed in by civil servants, even those at very senior levels with a maximum of a few years in a specialist area. An applicant for a very senior post in the DfE was told that their application was not being shortlisted, although 'you were clearly one of the strongest educationalists' who applied. In England, unlike Singapore, education experience is valued less highly than civil service experience.

We are currently in a good period when the DfE has established a strong operational group in each region of the country to identify and support academy trusts that are able to achieve school improvement. In 2023 they developed an algorithm to justify their decisions on selecting appropriate trusts to take on specific troubled schools. It was supposed to help civil servants understand the range of information about trusts. Of course, this algorithm could only take them so far ... and is limited by methodology issues such as how far past performance can predict future results.

The DfE has a huge amount of data. It has also developed good protocols for researchers to access and analyse this data. An interesting feature of the internal analyses of the DfE is what they tell us about different places in the country and the relative strengths and weaknesses of the school system. In 2016, there was a brave attempt to identify areas with the poorest social mobility and how they could be supported to improve educational standards. Policy evolved very rapidly around how these improvements should happen. Initially, these areas were both given additional funding for locally developed projects and were prioritised for every initiative in which the DfE was involved. However, this initiative was undermined by overload and weak implementation of any of the strategies suggested. A more successful later iteration gave greater ownership to each area of the improvements that had been identified and introduced independent chairs of partnership boards that oversaw the use of additional funding. The DfE focus on place later moved on to publishing area-based plans that identified 'cold spots' where more high-quality trusts were needed to provide support to poor schools struggling to improve.

First-time visitors to the London office of the DfE are advised to arrive early and have plenty of time in the waiting room. One wall is adorned by photographs of all the former secretaries of state for education and visitors will enjoy spotting the familiar pictures of Margaret Thatcher and Kenneth Clarke as well as marvelling at the five individuals who held the role in 2022 alone (including Michelle Donelan … for 36 hours). The other excitement of spending time in the waiting room is to watch and see who else is passing through!

At its best, the DfE can be a great enabler of improvement for children's education. At its worst, it fails to hold its nerve when influential voices rail against reasonable accountability mechanisms and systems. Few ministers have fully exploited the potential of their own personal position or realised how powerful their voices could have been if they were to have travelled much more extensively and set out a national vision for school improvement.

In any list of the most memorable secretaries of state it would be difficult not to include the following four (with an honourable mention for a minister who was never secretary of state but arguably had a much more positive influence than most who were):

- **Rab Butler**. Although looked down on by Churchill as an appeaser, Butler pushed through the decisive Education Act of 1944 (during wartime!).
- **Kenneth Baker**. Baker took the education baton from Callaghan and through the Education Reform Act in 1988 introduced a National Curriculum, the national assessments that became SATs, and Ofsted. The 'Baker days' for school staff professional development were named in his memory.
- **David Blunkett**. Blunkett made Blair's 1997 'education, education, education' commitment a reality.
- **Michael Gove**. Gove took the Labour Government's limited introduction of academies and nationalised the idea.
- **Nick Gibb**. While Gibb was never a secretary of state, he championed research on the effective teaching of early reading and transformed expectations of teaching synthetic phonics to young children.

The DfE is identified by whichever politician is currently heading it up, and the commitment by civil servants is to serve the elected government of the day. Within the DfE, however, there have been outstanding members of staff who have offered transformational advice and succeeded in having it heeded and acted on. Most of these have never become household names, even amongst the education intelligentsia. However, civil servants also have the ability to junk even the policies they have helped ministers painstakingly develop should political circumstances require it. Prior to the 2015 election – just nine months after the introduction of Regional School Commissioners – three draft letters were prepared for an incoming secretary of state, depending on the outcome of the election. Two included, 'Regional School Commissioners will immediately be abolished and their role brought to a summary end'. The third, however, stated 'The highly effective and innovative policy of introducing the role of Regional School Commissioners will be developed further with additional responsibilities for school improvement.'

ASIDE

Civil service values

When dealing with the DfE it is important to understand the working culture of the Civil Service.

Civil servants are appointed on merit on the basis of fair and open competition and are expected to carry out their roles with dedication and a commitment to the service's core values of integrity, honesty, objectivity and impartiality.

- **Integrity** puts the obligations of public service above personal interests.
- **Honesty** is being truthful and open.
- **Objectivity** is basing advice and decisions on rigorous analysis of the evidence.
- **Impartiality** is acting solely according to the merits of the case and serving governments of different political persuasions equally well.

These core values support good government and ensure the achievement of the highest possible standards in all that the Civil Service does. This in turn helps the Civil Service to gain and retain the respect of ministers, Parliament, the public, and its customers.

EXECUTIVES

The term 'executive head' has no consistent and commonly agreed usage. It has generally come to mean someone who is in charge of more than one school but even that is not always the case. The role of executive head often comes about when an existing head of a successful school is urgently needed to oversee another school that is encountering major difficulties. For example, when a school has had a terrible inspection outcome, then those responsible for the school may decide that the current headteacher either needs replacing or needs the assistance of someone with greater experience and skills. In this situation a common response is to ask a highly successful local headteacher to take the reins. Often this successful headteacher is not in a position to leave their current school and so an arrangement is reached where they are put in charge of both that school and the one in difficulties.

To carry out this strategy successfully generally requires the appointment of two senior staff as leaders who can be in charge at each school when the newly appointed executive head teacher is not on site. All kinds of different terms are used for these roles but 'head of school' is the most common.

In 2009, a catholic primary school in Camden was judged 'inadequate' and the experienced head of another catholic primary school in the borough became executive head across both schools. In 2010, both schools were inspected on the same day – the first school was judged 'outstanding' on the same day the second school came out of special measures. Fast forward to 2023, both schools are 'outstanding' and the school leader is now an executive leader across nine schools. The inexperienced head who was leading the school when it was judged inadequate in 2009, asked to be deputy to the new executive head.

She was part of the improvement journey and went on to be a head again in her own right at another school.

An executive head brings years of experience to their new school. Their job is to ensure improvement happens at a much faster rate than is likely to be the case with a raw headteacher. He or she will likely be transplanting procedures and practices that they have implemented at their successful school to the unsuccessful school as the fastest way to improve the latter. Key early challenges for the executive head include clearly setting out the relative responsibilities for each of the heads of school, how they will spend their own week, and the extent to which this is planned on a regular calendar each week. Balancing the time they spend between the two schools they are now responsible for is particularly important, as the new, unsuccessful, school could probably drink up every single minute of their time.

Some executive heads thrive even better in this role than they did as headteachers. They understand how to get the best from the leaders they appoint to each specific area within their schools. Many executive heads will lead two schools for as long a period as their careers allow or until it is time to move on to another demanding role.

There are some executive heads who are eventually able to take on a third school. At this stage, an executive headteacher really has moved away from the day-to-day work of each school. Their role becomes highly strategic and focuses on how to make the best use of the available leadership capacity across their group of schools. It is also likely that they will have made appointments which have responsibility across the group of schools. A major challenge for executive head teachers is when the head of a school that they have responsibility for faces crises that they struggle to cope with. In these situations, there is no alternative but for the executive head to get stuck in. However, implementation is crucial. The executive head needs to work alongside the head of school so that each crisis can be a learning experience.

A particularly interesting version of an executive headship role is when a regular head also has some wider involvement in one or more other schools, perhaps across a group of schools, such as a multi-academy trust. This strategy makes good use of heads who are already highly experienced and looking for more responsibility, but not yet ready to move away from day-to-day school leadership work. Such arrangements are best set up with a specific timescale and flexibility about the expectations so that the executive head's capacity is used to the full.

Do good heads make good executive heads? The skills required from an executive head include a very strong understanding of headship – and indeed successful experience of headship – but also an ability to work through others and allow them to grow in their work even if some of that work is not yet polished. Delegation is key.

Successful heads have found a way that worked in their first school. Executive headship builds on that experience but also requires the capacity to reflect on different circumstances and the need for new tactics in other situations. Executive headship calls for careful judgement over when and where to focus and get personally involved. An executive headship might seem a higher paid and less stressful role. However, in reality, it is a tougher job where you are accountable for more than one school, and the actions of less experienced and less skilled members of staff.

There are schools that need one leader. These leaders should not feel that they are not as valued and important as the executive heads who have moved on to take on responsibility across more than one school. In 2017, a school in a coastal town was judged 'inadequate' (having never in its history been judged better than 'requires improvement'). By 2019, it had been moved to a different academy trust. This trust recognised that an executive head from a successful school alone would not add sufficient additional capacity to improve the school rapidly. Consequently, they brought in not only the head of a highly successful school, but also very explicitly strengthened staffing and governance by bringing in several staff from the successful school and the chair of the local governing body.

Setting up arrangements for executive heads requires engaging carefully with the potential candidate's current school community. Initially there may be significant concerns from the staff, parents, and in particular governors, about the perceived loss of their headteacher. Indeed, governors may actively resist this development and will need reassurance that their school will continue to be in good hands. One strategy is to explain that this arrangement can be the best of both worlds, i.e. it is a new opportunity for the headteacher, without the school simply losing their valued leader as would be the case if the individual in question decided move on.

ASIDE

An executive head's impact

The right head or executive head can have a dramatic impact on a school. These two quotes are taken from the reports of two schools led by the same person – head at one school, and executive head at the other – both of which were inspected on the same day.

'The driving force behind the school's success is undoubtedly the gifted and dedicated headteacher.'

'The exceptional focus of the executive headteacher on improving teaching is reaping rich rewards for pupils.'

FORENSIC

School improvement is about getting every detail right. The serious school leader pays attention to every aspect of school life and focuses on improving it and aiming for excellence.

One of the marks of the successful school leader is a forensic attention to detail. They will look closely and carefully at every aspect of a particular issue, analyse data, and only agree on interpretations after much consideration. While much of a school leader's work is relational, motivational, and relentless, bringing a forensic mindset to bear ensures that actions towards improvement are focused and thoughtful.

When a school is doing very poorly, it's not difficult for any school leader – or even occasional visitor or parent – to see that there is much to do to put things right. As schools improve, and, on the surface at least start operating at a moderately successful level, it becomes a more sophisticated task to assess and analyse strengths and areas for further development.

National surveys of opinions about behaviour in schools show that perceptions can be very different across the same school. In general, headteachers are the most positive overall about behaviour, with staff a little less positive, then parents, and children by far the least positive. These opinions reflect relative experiences. While headteachers may be aware of incidents of poor behaviour, they may be comforted by knowing that these are fairly rare and are not the experience of the vast majority of children across the school. For staff in classrooms – where these incidents of poor behaviour generally occur – the fact that they are rare is of little help in the moment. This is the case also for children in these classes and the parents when their children report misbehaviour to their families.

Discussions about behaviour need to move beyond a focus on maintaining order and a polite demeanour among students to the effectiveness of the culture for learning across the school. There may be only a small amount of low level, poor behaviour, but for lessons where it does take place it is deeply destructive to the pace of learning for the children in those classes. School leaders need to set themselves the same thresholds and expectations as the children in the school have and be ferocious and forensic about addressing where there is any poor behaviour across the school.

It is best to establish clear data collection mechanisms to help understand the extent and impact of misbehaviour. This is perhaps particularly important when on the surface behaviour appears much improved. At the beginning of each school year leaders should work hard to reset staff and student expectations; how children will be encouraged to meet these expectations; and, where necessary, the sanctions that will accompany non-compliance. The best school leaders will also spend several weeks reinforcing the different routines and behaviour that are expected during lessons, at moments of transition, and during break periods. They will ensure they collect data on instances of poor behaviour, whether this is improving, and where there may be specific parts of the school which need further specific attention.

A key task for all school leaders is to ensure that the school has a highly effective curriculum. Much work will go into setting out plans which provide continuity and effective sequencing across the school. This will be accompanied by professional development for staff on the implementation of these plans and ensuring that staff understand their key features. However, if a school leader believes their job is now completed, they are sadly misguided. While brilliant curriculum plans can lead to astonishing and effective lessons, they can also be completely massacred in the hands of a poor teacher.

The school leader needs to know how their plans work in practice for children in each classroom. School leaders need to understand both the devil in the detail of individual lessons and how the overall week maps out for children, whether the time allocated to each subject is appropriate and whether the links that can be made between subjects are fully exploited. This is not straightforward and requires a school leader to have a structure for curriculum leadership that is shared amongst the senior staff of the school. Senior staff need to share understandings and expectations of the plans which have been put in place and how they will be implemented.

Any decent school will have many wider opportunities for the children. Some of these will be part of the school's curriculum offer and involve visits, speakers, and a wide variety of resource material that helps bring the curriculum to life. There will also be extracurricular activities where children will have a measure of choice about those that they wish to take up. School leaders need to be alive to the consequences of choice and to ensure that it does not reinforce the advantages some children coming to school already have over their less fortunate peers.

Music can be a great outlet for children. There are many children who are less successful in other areas of school life, or who are not always onboard with what school is trying to teach them, who come to life in music. Whatever capacity a school has for a range of work in music it should be able to provide children with a great singing diet.

Best practice is to facilitate a wide range of exciting opportunities but also to monitor participation. Do boys join the school choir? Do girls get the same opportunities for team sports? Do those who love sport without being very good at it also get the opportunity to participate, and not just with their friends but in competitive matches with other schools? Tracking participation by individuals but also by the key characteristics of children is essential for the school which aims to be inclusive.

Hopefully a school leader will be able to put together a team of trusted colleagues with the skills needed for the school improvement journey. For this team to operate at maximum effectiveness there needs to be clarity over the role of each member. In many cases these members hold other senior responsibilities, and the school leader needs to ensure that there is clarity around each role and where responsibility for each area lies. This requires detailed planning – not just casual conversations conducted in school corridors.

There are many areas of school life that benefit from a detailed forensic approach. While a detailed discussion is beyond the scope of this chapter, a few key areas that require forensic gathering and analysis of data are:

- **The analysis of attainment data**. Are there positive trends overall? Are individual children achieving what the teacher believed was possible at the beginning of the year? What are the characteristics of those children who do not achieve well?

- **Equality, diversity, and inclusion**. Without data on each protected characteristic, an espoused commitment is little more than words.

- **Recruitment**. Staff recruitment should be rigorous, test applicants fully on all aspects of the job specification, and follow up references fully. It should not simply be based on first impressions in the interview.

A forensic approach is a professional approach. There are many aspects of school leadership that can be enjoyable in themselves, are fulfilling, or lead to improvement. However, there are also many aspects which are gruelling, relentless, frustrating, and demanding of a school leader's time. The temptation to cut corners is ever present. Indeed, a school leader's time *is* finite and rational choices *do* need to be made about how best to use it. However, unless school improvement tasks are phased and implemented carefully, they will have to be repeated and take yet more time.

Just as the successful athlete knows that their success is based on the hard training that took place through the cold dark winter, so it is for the school leader. Success in school improvement is based on hours and hours of relentless and forensic activity.

ASIDE

New South Wales school inspections

The format and aims of school inspections vary across the world, here is a summary of the system in New South Wales. Looking at systems such as this one can give us insight into areas in which we should forensically collect data within our own schools.

In 2023, 30 schools were chosen at random. Inspectors contacted the selected principals at least four school days before the inspection. Schools were inspected in relation to:

- Child Protection.
- Alignment of curriculum documentation and expectations in Human Society and its Environment (Primary Schools).
- Alignment of curriculum documentation and expectations in Science (Secondary Schools).
- Assessment policies and procedures (Secondary Schools, 16-18 year olds).

The inspection considered the context in which these schools operate as members of a system and the associated responsibilities of the system in managing compliance. Where a random inspection identified compliance concerns, the school and, if relevant, the system, were requested to provide further evidence addressing these concerns.

GOVERNANCE

For many school leaders, governance does not figure as prominently as it should in their school improvement toolbox. As a new head, there can be a determination to see off any challenge, including from well-meaning trustees or governors. A head can always use their higher level of knowledge to see off any meaningful challenge from the board. However, this encourages trustees and governors to become a passive supporters' club rather than acting as the accountable body they should be.

When school leaders embrace governance they become better leaders. There can be a temptation for headteachers to think that at long last they are in charge and can lead in the way they have always hoped to. In reality, everyone is accountable and nobody's leadership should be entirely unfettered. The wise school leader will take their accountability to trustees or governors seriously and will in turn find their ideas honed and their focus sharpened. Experienced school leaders and governors can help less sure footed headteachers understand the positive impact of governance. When functioning correctly governance transforms from the chair simply working through an agenda to supporting the headteacher to finesse the school improvement plan, its implementation, speed, and impact.

School leaders generally get the governance and trustees or governors they deserve.

When the headteacher gives the governors or trustees an opportunity to influence the school and make a difference, then they will find that papers will be read in advance and considered carefully. The chair will run the meeting rather than just reading the agenda and announcing the next item. If you make time in the meeting for governors and trustees – rather than school leaders – to decide what should be discussed and how to prioritise time, then they will be invested and engaged in these meetings.

This requires school leaders to be relaxed about not being in control.

Weak governance is marked by:

- School leaders talking far too much.
- School leaders using acronyms and when asked about these, spending disproportionate time explaining their meaning.
- Trustees or governors coming unprepared and reading the papers at the meeting.
- Questions from trustees or governors receiving perfunctory responses that fail to explore the point that was being raised.

Effective governance is marked by clarity and focus on *the main thing*. The main thing is children doing better, achieving more, and experiencing more. With focus and clarity the agenda, the information needed to support discussion, and the follow up actions required will fall into place.

Indicators of effective governance include:

- How difficult points raised by a trustee or governor are received. If school leaders respond defensively, then even conscientious trustees and governors think twice before asking questions that may be perceived as awkward. The mark of a school leader determined to see improvement will be to embrace awkward questions and do their best to understand and engage with points made, however tangential they may initially seem.
- A plan of what is to be achieved should be at the top of every agenda, e.g. results improved by x% by next summer, school ready to be judged 'good' in eighteen months, behaviour to be exemplary in two terms, etc.
- The trustees and governors should shape the agenda, and, once papers have been circulated, decide on priorities.

- Allowing for different kinds of discussion. These include getting through the agenda, whatever needs to be approved, and also having extended periods to consider progress in key areas.

- Senior leaders beyond the head should present at meetings. Trustees and governors will come to understand the strengths and development needs of these senior leaders who in turn will experience the challenges of governance and better understand the goals to which they are being expected to work.

- Papers should be short. 'If I had more time, I would have written a shorter letter' should apply to school leaders. Few things are more daunting for trustees and governors than long, impenetrable, reports with such extensive data that it is impossible to see the wood for the trees.

- Making clear what the point of a papers is. Is it to inform a decision? To comment on? Trustees and governors are not there to be entertained by school leaders, but to check the progress on making the school great – from whatever position it is at currently.

Governance papers are now provided to trustees and governors electronically. A helpful way for school leaders to collect papers in preparation for a meeting can be to use some kind of portal. Trustees and governors can then access papers for the meeting but also quickly locate information from previous meetings should that be helpful. However, for busy trustees and governors, thoughtful school leaders will consider carefully how best to present not just individual papers but also the complete pack. Much can be learnt from the care with which local authority committee clerks provide papers for council members for the range of meetings they attend.

A key but sometimes awkward question is how should trustees and governors know what to believe, e.g. whether behaviour is improving as the data presented by school leaders indicates or whether there still remain significant concerns as continually mentioned by parent governors. School leaders need to agree with trustees or governors on when to commission external reviews of particular aspects of what needs improving in a school. Crucially – while the reviewer will work with school leaders while conducting their review – those with responsibility for governance should arrange how they receive feedback directly from the reviewer.

Throughout this chapter, the term trustees or governors has been studiously used to refer to both school governing bodies and academy trust trustees. An academy trust is likely to be responsible for a number of schools. A trust board has a number of responsibilities. These include to ensure that the trust is in good health financially, has mechanisms to keep abreast of monthly management accounts, and has strong audit processes in place – including a robust committee and probing internal and external audit reports. However, the main purpose of an academy trust board is to ensure that every school in its care provides effectively for its children and is on a constant improvement path. This requires different mechanisms to those of single school governing bodies and care needs to be given maintaining the appropriate level of scrutiny.

Key to all of this is the accountability of the chief executive to the trust board and how information is provided to the latter. In general, in an academy trust, a senior trust leader will line manage a school's headteacher. Once a trust has more than, say, four schools, a trust board will not review the kind of details that a school governing body would expect to, e.g. mathematics attainment in Year 4. A key part of a trust board's responsibilities is making clear how this kind of detail will continue to be scrutinised, by who, and what the mechanisms are for giving assurance that this is being carried out. Two possible approaches are:

- The chief executive or key central trust staff (the latter of whom report to the chief executive), are responsible for overseeing the school governing body as well as line managing headteachers.
- The trust board receives assessments of the work of school governing bodies as part of reports on the progress of each school.

ASIDE

Foreword to a trust governor handbook

The key principles of governance in this trust are:

- Children come first in every decision.
- No challenge that drives improvement is too great.
- Making remarkable change happen.

Governors are one of the largest volunteer forces in the country and have an important part to play in raising academy standards. The role of the local governing board is one of the keys to the effectiveness of an academy.

Governors and teachers share the same values, face similar issues, and are geographically close enough to support and challenge each other. Both of us recognise the unique characteristics of each of the communities in which we work and how they are reflected in our distinctive school cultures. We encourage cultural diversity, celebrate the special qualities of each of our schools, and recognise that for communities to become sustainable they must develop and grow. We look for what works and make sure that all the children in our trust learn from that knowledge. We are working towards a partnership that respects, sustains, and supports. Our model is about creating interdependence. We subscribe to a set of shared values, principles, and operational processes that ensure quality education for all our young people.

Our central belief is that every young life is special, open to possibility, gifted with the potential to change the world for the better but also bound by the limits of their own circumstances. Our ambition is to unlock the potential of all children, remove the barriers to their aspirations and ensure that all our children succeed. Governors play a key role in the success of our academies and the trust as a whole. We are proud to support them in their roles.

HEADTEACHERS

Headteachers are the most important people in a school's improvement journey. But not all heads are suited to every school improvement journey. There are specific attributes that a head requires to lead a successful school improvement journey.

Heads need to be brave; but not rash. Bravery is about making the right decisions despite the consequences. It is about calling out behaviour that is unacceptable whosoever is responsible for it. It is about siding with children rather than staff. It is about sticking with staff who you are convinced have the right values even after they have made mistakes. It is fronting up to the most uncomfortable situations and returning rudeness with professionalism.

School leaders may not feel brave – they may well be scared of heights, be privately anxious, doubt their own abilities, or feel they lack the charisma and bravura they admire in other colleagues. However, these are not the qualities school leaders need. What *is* needed is the confidence and then the determination to 'do the right thing' and stay the course through the most difficult bits of a school's improvement journey.

Heads also need to be honest. There are times as a school leader when telling the truth is not easy, when it is tempting to avoid admitting to things that have gone wrong or confronting problems. True honesty, however, is much more than this. It is being prepared to be completely frank about the state of the education that children at a school are being provided. It is being able to tell colleagues – in a constructive and kind way – where their practice needs to improve.

Honesty is about a school leader's own performance too. When a school leader is able to see their own strengths but also identify areas where they are less well-developed, the pace of their own development will accelerate. When school leaders model this kind of professional honesty it will be taken up by senior staff and others across the school.

If there is one characteristic that school leaders need above all others it is surely integrity. Integrity is walking the walk as well as talking the talk – to be true to your word and totally reliable. There are many pressures on school leaders, their time, their thinking, and their priorities. School leaders are tested on how they handle these pressures with integrity. A school leader's integrity is particularly challenged when the school performs poorly or when an individual behaves in a way that does not meet the school's standards. Taking criticism on the chin and getting to grips with whatever has gone wrong is not easy. However, in the long term it is always better to face the music; maintaining denial will erode trust in the school, without resolving the issue at hand (which will in any case have to be faced eventually).

A school leader needs to narrate the school improvement journey so that everyone – staff, parents, and all connected with the school – understand and are encouraged by the steps being taken. However, no matter how positive the story the school leader is able to tell, it is crucial that they do not get carried away by their own publicity. School leaders will not have reached their leadership role without both personal confidence and ambition. However, those that are able to maintain their humility have a greater chance of inspiring their colleagues to achieve what is needed.

Humility does not equate to meekness or a lack of assertiveness. It does not mean a reluctance to delegate or maintain expectations of colleagues. Humility will manifest in different ways but will often be accompanied by a lack of airs and graces and a willingness to take part in the difficult elements of school life.

While integrity is the most desirable characteristic in school leaders, good communication skills are also needed. We have all seen the results of poor communication. When school leaders pay insufficient attention to internal communication then staff are left unclear about expectations and procedures, and senior staff end up unable to manage their time and become overstretched. Most school leaders also need to develop their skills in external communication, particularly with parents. External communication can rarely be too frequent, but it is also critical to maintain a tone that is suitably assuring without being patronising. To develop and improve these communication skills requires both effort and taking on board feedback.

School leaders inherit their staff. It is the leader's role to enable this group of staff to do better than they have done previously. In time, vacancies will arise, and a school leader needs to take these opportunities; two years into a leadership role a leader's team should be stronger than the one they inherited. Sometimes there are very specific challenges, as some of the best staff will be those who move on to promoted posts. Leading recruitment processes with rigour is essential. Simply putting out an advertisement to attract the staff that the school needs to take it forward is relying on luck. Busy as they are, school leaders also need to spend time looking outwards and finding staff seeking fresh opportunities – so that when a vacancy appears, the school leader has people to whom the advertisement can be sent. This is an area where an effective trust can really support new heads.

School leaders have a lot of discretion about how to spend their time but also many demands upon it. Some days they will come in with a long list of tasks and go home having hardly looked at it because of situations that have arisen during the day to which they have had to give their attention.

Despite these demands on their time, great headteachers teach. They model what matters. School leaders should not have reached their exalted position without a very successful earlier career that will have included being a very good teacher. Continuing to teach is an opportunity to model best practice to colleagues and keep a hand in the day-to-day operation of the school. School leaders that do this, however, do face challenges, particularly in keeping to timetabled commitments when other pressing engagements can arise at any time and on any day. Further, school leaders that continue to teach but are too busy to plan, mark, or liaise effectively, are not modelling the kind of teaching they undoubtedly expect from their colleagues.

Headteachers have different personalities, and some will find the demands of being in the public eye more challenging than others. Whether it comes naturally or not, being prepared to speak publicly is crucial. Communities are quick to judge and will have all kinds of expectations of a headteacher. Most of all they will look to see whether a new headteacher looks the part. Some headteachers will find the demands of the local press excruciating, while others will adapt quickly. It is essential that headteachers quickly get over any reluctance to have their photograph taken. Of course, they will want children to feature in great stories about the school ... but communities associate schools with figureheads and effective headteachers need to be those figureheads. Sometimes this can jar with heads who have a humble approach. However, while humility is a virtue, fronting up to this aspect of the job is crucial in giving confidence to the community.

This chapter has been about the many demands on headteachers and the expectation that they can manage them all. However, to be successful a headteacher very definitely needs to be selective with the tasks they take on. Headteachers who try to do it all will find three problems:

- They will not have time to perform everything well.
- Nobody else will learn the tasks that the headteacher keeps to themselves.
- The school will miss out because undoubtedly there will be some aspects of what the headteacher has been doing that someone else would do much better.

ASIDE

Headteachers' Standards in England

The following is taken from the government guidance document *Headteachers' Standards 2020 in England* (https://www.gov.uk/government/publications/national-standards-of-excellence-for-headteachers/headteachers-standards-2020).

Headteachers are leading professionals and role models for the communities they serve. Their leadership is a significant factor in ensuring high quality teaching and achievement in schools and a positive and enriching experience of education for pupils. Together with those responsible for governance, they are custodians of the nation's schools.

Parents and the wider public rightly hold high expectations of headteachers, given their influential position leading the teaching profession and over the young people who are their responsibility.

Headteachers are expected to demonstrate consistently high standards of principled and professional conduct.

Headteachers uphold public trust in school leadership and maintain high standards of ethics and behaviour.

Standards cover:

1. School culture.
2. Teaching.
3. Curriculum and assessment.
4. Behaviour.
5. Additional and special educational needs.
6. Professional development.
7. Organisational management.
8. School improvement.
9. Working in partnership.
10. Governance and accountability.

INTERIMS

Interim boards are one of the most underused resources in school improvement. They are a way to move responsibility for achieving school improvement from the individual head to a collective body.

The tactic comes from the long-standing legislation about 'schools causing concern' that predates the academy movement. When a school reached a serious level of concern it was possible for a local authority to withdraw the delegated powers of a governing body and for the local authority to establish an Interim Executive Board. All three words matter. It is an interim or temporary arrangement lasting only as long as is needed for the school to cease causing concern. It has executive powers in that it is a group that makes decisions. And it is a board, that is a group, who work together to accelerate school improvement.

The IEB as originally envisaged is now rare, as remaining local authority maintained schools that become a cause for concern are generally now considered to need to join an academy trust. They may still be used in areas still resistant to academisation. Much more commonplace, though, is an evolution of the concept to the academy context. Governance in academy trusts is much less rule-driven than in local authority maintained schools – it is the responsibility of academy trusts to ensure successful school improvement and the tools to achieve this are in their own hands. What has emerged as effective practice is the use of interim boards when a school needs a kick up the proverbial backside to see very rapid progress. In practice this can happen in a variety of ways.

In many cases an interim board replaces the usual local governance arrangement a trust will generally have for each school. In other cases, it operates as part of those local governance arrangements, for example, as a committee. An advantage of this version of interim boards is that they focus solely on school improvement – leaving aside the other 'usual' matters that the wider local governance arrangements are responsible for. In these cases, the interim board may be referred to as a 'Standards Committee' or something similar.

The key feature of an interim board is that it holds school leaders accountable to the school improvement plan, while also holding those charged with supporting leadership accountable for that support. An interim board is generally very small – typically three or four non-executives – and should not be made up of either school leaders or the key staff supporting the school leaders. The school improvement plan includes all the actions that will be needed to move the school from its current position to providing an education that all involved can be proud of. This will include the school finances, the state of the school building, urgent HR issues, suitable IT equipment and infrastructure, necessary recruitment, and the school's safeguarding arrangements, as well as its classroom practices.

The first task of an interim board is to accept an improvement plan that covers all areas that need addressing across the school. The second task is to draw up an agenda that requires different people to report on progress in the improvement areas for which they are responsible. The third task is to track the agreed actions and ensure that every action is discussed fortnightly until it has been completed.

Academy trusts that operate interim boards can face dilemmas over membership of these boards. The most effective people at the school are likely to already be on the trust board and so it is tempting for them to roll up their sleeves and bring their skills to accelerating improvement. This is tricky as the trust board will need to keep an oversight of all school improvement and remain able to judge the effectiveness of its various strategies – it will also have the right to bring a particular ineffective strategy to a conclusion. This will be harder if some members of the interim board are personally invested in those strategies, for example as part of the trust board.

A great aspect of interim boards is that the norm for how many people might typically be thought to be needed to form say a governing body or a trust board goes out the window. Experience is clear that three or four serious and committed members is both sufficient and efficient in terms of time and capacity.

To run effectively interim boards need:

- Well-prepared and clear papers circulated in advance so that discussion focusses on evaluating issues rather than introducing them.
- Papers prepared by all staff, not just school leaders, and accountability for that reporting.
- Fortnightly hour-long meetings.
- A culture where challenges and critical questions are welcomed and engaged with.
- Agreed actions that are followed up remorselessly.
- Each meeting to include a review of the big picture. Is the school making progress in the timescale expected?
- Well-clerked minutes. These should not be produced by a member of the interim board or school leader.

There is always a temptation to bring the work of interim boards to a close too soon. A school may be working towards an inspection schedule; though that precise schedule is of course always a matter of guesswork until the call the day before an inspection. The intensity of effort required makes an interim board hard to sustain, but careful thought is needed when it approaches the end of its operation. Is some kind of phased ending needed to ensure that the usual governance arrangements pick up the pace?

A wonderful development in the academy world is the generosity of trusts in supporting each other through senior executives of one serving on the interim board of another. This has benefits for all involved – the senior executive leader from one trust sees improvement strategies up close, without the same level of involvement, and the recipient trust gains external scrutiny, with no conflicts of interest, to judge the extent of the school's progress.

Many trusts have established Standards Committees that report to their Trust Boards and review school improvement work. These have immense potential but also several risks. In the worst case the committee is ineffective while the board feels absolved of any concerns about school improvement. In the best case they widen the board's understanding of what progress can look like, and how fast progress is actually happening. Again, there is an opportunity for these committees to have external membership, and these external members can bring a degree of challenge that insiders from the trust central team are unlikely to be able to provide.

ASIDE

Interim boards

Interim boards can make a real difference to school improvement. Consider this quote from an inspection report of a school that had been previously judged inadequate:

> 'Trustees responded rapidly and robustly to the findings from Ofsted's last monitoring visit. The interim executive board has sharply held leaders to account, while also making sure that leaders have the support to make a difference. The quality of provision is better, and systems are stronger.'

JEREMY

This is the story of Jeremy's journey. Jeremy was an excellent teacher, who everyone said was a rising star. He had a way with children that meant he was loved by both them and their parents. He was admired by most of his colleagues, even if some of the most experienced teachers felt a slight jealousy that it had taken them many more years to gain the kind of credibility that seemed to come so effortlessly to Jeremy. In what seemed no time at all he was given early responsibilities, and he began to discuss with senior colleagues the possibility of a long career.

Jeremy was happy at his school without yet being aware that it was actually not very well-functioning. Although he flourished, this was because of his innate talent, and he received little support in his role as the school was, to put it mildly, in a bit of a mess. As Jeremy started his third year at the school, he began to be aware of some disquiet. Initially he was sufficiently self-contained to keep away from the rather uncomfortable gossip that was increasingly part of the staffroom discourse. However, in time, the conversations became part of the more formal school staff meetings.

One morning there was a message that there was to be an emergency additional staff briefing before school. The headteacher, clearly flustered, and reading from a piece of paper, announced that the deputy headteacher had left the school and would not be returning. She went on to say that there should be no discussion about the matter. Furthermore, she was to be told immediately should any member of staff be approached by the press, and there was certainly to be no conversation about this with any parent or governor.

The staff had no time to digest the announcement as the school day was about to start and each of them was needed in their own classroom.

As Jeremy pondered the matter, he was torn between feeling concerned for what the future held for the former deputy headteacher, and reflecting that the truth was that the man was not really up to the job. What he had not bargained for, however, was the headteacher asking to speak to him at lunchtime and asking him immediately to be the interim acting deputy headteacher.

Jeremy tried to ask a bit about what would be expected of him ... the headteacher, however, was more focused on what leadership point Jeremy would expect to be paid at and making it clear that the role was only for a temporary period. Jeremy sat down that evening and decided he would be the very best deputy head he could possibly be even if it turned out to be only very briefly. Over the coming weeks he threw himself into the role. He was worried that his colleagues would consider him an upstart ... but he quickly learned that three more experienced members of staff had been offered the role and turned it down. Within a few weeks his colleagues were giving him great feedback and saying that he was the deputy head the school had needed for a long time. Jeremy found he relished leadership. He enjoyed sorting out difficulties and was rather pleased with himself when he found he was actually quite good at what the headteacher expected of him.

A further term went by. Then one Monday morning, just as the classes were due to go into their usual assembly, the school secretary ran into his classroom. He knew immediately that there was a problem having never seen her outside her office before. In a loud whisper she said to him, 'Take the assembly – Ofsted is on the phone.'

The next few days passed in a blur. The inspectors arrived, the school had a very rough time and was judged to be very poor, and two days later the headteacher called in sick. No one was very clear about what was meant to happen next or who was in charge but Jeremy gradually learnt that their school was to join an academy trust ... he was sort of in charge for the next few weeks but shortly after that another head would be parachuted into the school. Although Jeremy had heard of such changes to schools, he was never given a proper explanation of what it all meant, or what the implications were for a temporary interim acting deputy headteacher.

At the start of the following term, a new head was in place and set out a clear improvement plan to get the school back on the straight and narrow, and also satisfy Ofsted at a later visit. Jeremy hoped for the best and could see that change was needed, given the previous school leader's lack of success. But what happened was that things got worse – several of the staff most loved by parents did not appreciate the new regime and found jobs elsewhere. The school found it hard to recruit replacements and several classes were taught by supply teachers, some of whom had patchy attendance. And to cap it all, the new head announced at the end of her first term that she had landed a job in an international school and would be leaving immediately.

For a second time, Jeremy found himself leading the school, having neither sought the role nor having been selected and appointed to it. This time there was no new head brought in. The new trust seemed very distant, emails went without reply, and there was a parent petition blaming the trust for the school being in such a terrible state.

A couple of weeks into the term, someone from the trust central office visited. They did not speak with any of the other staff except for an hour with Jeremy, during which they asked a lot of questions that he was not able to answer. What progress had there been with the post-inspection action plan? What recruitment had there been to fill vacancies? How was Jeremy going to address the deficit that had occurred in the school's finances? Jeremy asked what support he might expect from the trust, and when he might find out about his own future as a school leader? He was told that it would depend on how these pressing issues were addressed.

Jeremy resigned and began talking with his friends about what alternative careers he might pursue. Behind the scenes, unbeknown to Jeremy, there was light at the end of the tunnel. The trust that had taken on the school made at least one correct decision. They accepted that they had bitten off more than they could chew and welcomed an offer from another local trust to take on the school.

A month later – just as Jeremy was about to accept interviews for posts he had applied for abroad – a highly experienced head visited and asked to spend the day with him, observing the school and getting his take on what was needed. At the end of the day, this experienced head explained the change of trust that would take place, that she was to be a new executive head for the school, and that she hoped that she could persuade Jeremy to stay and take on the head of school role.

Jeremy was still early in his career and having seen ineffective leadership by both school and trust leaders, was much more jaded than the bright rising star of just a few years previously. Fortunately, he decided to accept the offer. The rest of his story is more cheerful. First, central involvement in an exciting school improvement journey that led to it being judged good in two years, and extremely good four years later. Then headship in another of the trust's schools. And then, five years later, to an executive headship. In time he even took a day each week as the lead mentor for all new heads across the trust.

Jeremy is a pseudonym and some details have been amended to provide anonymity. However, many will recognise aspects of this story in their own careers. Tragically, there are too many promising leaders who have not stayed in education because they did not meet the right leader/mentor/human being in time. There may be no silver bullets in school improvement, but there are also no lost causes.

ASIDE

Preparing for principalship, New Zealand

School systems across the world have different educational and organisational cultures, however, they often face similar issues and so there is much we can learn from others' approaches. Here are some recommendations for professional development and preparation towards a principalship taken from *Preparing and supporting new principals – a guide for aspiring and new principals* (2023), Available at: https://ero.govt.nz/our-research/preparing-and-supporting-new-principals-a-guide-for-aspiring-and-new-principals).

There are three broad stages of learning:

- Instructional leadership: Developing deep and comprehensive pedagogical knowledge is foundational. It is something you can begin early, as it is compatible with a teaching role.

- Higher-order and interpersonal skills: Developing skills such as strategic thinking, change leadership, and emotional and social intelligence, needs time. You should seek opportunities to do this before taking on the role of principal.

- Management abilities: Developing management knowledge and skills is best undertaken just before taking on a principal role so you can immediately consolidate your learning through practise.

KILLER

... INDICATORS

School leaders focus on improving the learning experience for children and making sure their staff have the skills to maximise those children's progress. This requires attention to the culture for learning in the school, a clear and progressive curriculum, and support for teachers with their pedagogy to make best use of every lesson. Alongside this, leaders will put in place mechanisms to assess and monitor the progress of the school's improvement plan, and of children's academic achievement as the key performance indicator of the school. The school leader will also be accountable for how all these are going to whoever has overall oversight – be it governors or a trust board (who should also support the leader with planning and assessment).

There are killer indicators that can help take a 'temperature check' of how a school is doing. These are useful for external visitors, but also any school leader interested in developing the ability to 'hover over' and take an impartial overview of their school as well as be in the thick of it. These indicators are not in themselves the most important factors in a school's improvement. However, lack of attention to them is a sure sign of a school leader not thinking broadly enough about the successful culture they are looking to embed across their school. They are pressure points, often in day-to-day, non-academic contexts, that reveal deeper stresses on the school.

A person who visits the school regularly will often arrive during the school day and sign in at the school's reception. Ideally, this encounter would be reassuring – a smile, a friendly word, and the impression of a school that is busy but on top of its day-to-day administration. Too often, though, school reception areas and the staff responsible for being the first face of the school attract less positive descriptions.

An assessor, or other regular external visitor, who is always used to receiving a slightly VIP welcome may need to see how others who arrive are treated. The least attractive trait is a receptionist who makes a point of needing to finish something else before paying attention to a visitor. Other unwelcoming features are a lack of patience and sympathy: asking questions that border on impatience, straying from explaining the school's policy on punctuality to being judgemental, agreeing to pass on a forgotten lunch box but in such a way to make clear that it really is over and above their role, and other behaviours that make parents feel a nuisance and unwelcome. Staff at reception are busy, and not everyone is at their best 100% of the time, but all of these reflect poorly on the school's culture.

In my career, an amazingly high proportion of my time has been taken up by phoning schools, nearly always hoping to talk with the headteacher, then leaving a message or arranging a time to phone again. Answers vary. Some are delightful, welcoming, and helpful (whether the headteacher happens to be available or not). With others … you try to learn the number to press that might avoid going through an automated list of the names and numbers of each head of year group as well as finance, admissions, the deputy head, the head's PA, the site manager, the deputy site manager, a special message about a forthcoming INSET day, and a reminder that attendance matters. By this time, one's mind wanders, you miss the option you need, and have to start over again. Once you finally get to a human voice, the real differences emerge. In some, the merest mention of the headteacher immediately raises the hackles. While some are happy to take a message, others will only take a name and say they will see if someone might return the call. Worst of all, however, is when the tone completely changes as soon as they think your job role is 'important' (the implication being, not one of the parental riff raff).

A school that empathises with parents is a humane school. Just as in the classroom, a good school sets clear expectations and is as consistent as possible in applying them (while allowing space for some individual accommodations). The same applies to the school's interactions with families: from the timing of daily routines such as the start and end of day, changes of clothes needed for physical exercise, to lunches, etc. The thinking school understands that everyone's lives have ups and downs, and that during the downs everyone needs kindness and sympathy.

Understanding families' lives gives staff a greater chance of reacting appropriately when children are out of sorts. However, staff who have a natural inclination to kindness and sympathy also need to know the limits of their expertise. When families present staff with unfamiliar challenges that they are not equipped to handle appropriately then they should be kind and sympathetic but also refer families to the appropriate professionals with the skills to provide the necessary support.

School leaders need to have a standard response to complaints – use the policy. Wise school leaders will look to avoid feelings, or indeed statements, of outrage at parents or others being so brazen to put in what some staff may think is clearly an entirely malicious complaint. School leaders are well-advised to take every complaint seriously. Staff, and school leaders themselves, need to understand that handling complaints is part of being a public service. Sometimes complaints are entirely justified, in which case it is important to take on whatever learning there is that arises from reviewing them.

An institution being ready to apologise goes a long way with some complainants. When there are lessons to be draw from a complaint then adjusting processes, procedures, and communications is relatively straightforward, but being prepared to change mindsets and attitudes is much harder. One of the roles of school leaders is to model any changes in mindset and attitude that may be necessary.

No school is set up, or suitably resourced, to meet the needs of every single child in the country, no matter what disability or special need they may have. But some schools live out their espoused commitments to inclusion by much more careful consideration of how they can adapt their practice and make adjustments to be suitable for a wider range of children. It is shocking that there continue to be school leaders who happily tell parents that a similar mainstream school down the road would be much more suitable for their child. As an indicator of a school leader who has lost sight of what their job is about, few are more telling than this.

Unfortunately, there are few ways to call this out. Unsurprisingly parents that experience this kind of attitude will rightly conclude that this school is unlikely to be suitable for their child.

Standing in the playground and observing as children arrive and leave school is very telling. The very presence of senior staff tells parents and pupils that senior leaders are accessible and that it is easy to go and talk to them, no matter how small the matter. A matter that seems small to school staff may be causing great anxiety in a family and sharing concern with the school can quickly reduce that worry.

If those with responsibility for oversight of a school discover that the school leader has been struggling for some time without this becoming apparent, then this should be the cause of some serious soul searching. Symptoms of struggling in this way include (but are not limited to) repeated cancellations or postponements of appointments or meetings with people outside the school, or a leader who was previously always on time with tasks becoming one who needs constant reminders. This isn't easy to tackle, as when a school leader is going through hard times, they need a bit of slack and understanding if they do not keep up with all expectations.

ASIDE

Indicator checklist

Can a school be a good school if:

- Staff can ring and leave a message without speaking to anyone to say they can't attend today.
- Parents who raise a concern do not get a phone call back the same day.
- There is an 'atmosphere' in the staffroom when the head walks in.
- It takes more than a day to book a conversation with a senior member of staff.
- The culture of classrooms does not look beyond a heavy focus on sanctions.
- Children with special educational needs get terrible exam results.
- 'What can you expect from these children?' is said by any member of staff.
- Litter is not quickly addressed.
- It does not have a library.
- School meals are unappetising.
- Handwriting and presentation are poor.
- Displays of children's work are poorly arranged.
- The school office phone rings more than three times before it is answered.
- Unsuccessful applicants are not offered and given feedback on their applications.
- Children watch films on the last day of term.
- Children do not have two hours each week of physical activity.
- There is no girls' football team.
- Spelling mistakes by staff go unaddressed.
- The headteacher looks miserable.
- Senior leaders think this list is a waste of time.

LONELINESS

School improvement is a team effort. No one can succeed in transforming a school on their own. The school leader charged with school improvement will have to decide which aspects they will personally lead and take responsibility for, but the much bigger task is to put together a team with the various skills and strengths needed to achieve the overall result. Each team operates differently – but a common thread in successful teams is a shared commitment that transcends individual responsibility and personal success or failure. The leader of a team bears responsibility for setting the tone and expectations, and encouraging its members through successes and setbacks.

A school leader also needs to be ready for intense periods of loneliness. This loneliness is often unseen by even close members of the team around the school leader. One of the dawning realisations of early headship is that it is unlike any other school leadership role previously encountered. This is even the case for those heads who have had the very best deputy headship experience and have benefitted from a close working relationship with a headteacher and mentor figure who has done everything they can to prepare their deputy.

Headship not only brings the responsibility of confidential knowledge, but a sharp realisation that the buck really does stop with you. No matter how much support, and careful induction is provided, a headteacher is very quickly either excited or appalled by the huge expectation and enormous responsibility that the role holds. When a new headteacher is also expected to lead significant school improvement, the excitement or horror is even greater. (As an aside, one of the areas selection panels for headships need to consider is whether the challenge will overwhelm a candidate or prompt greatness.)

Is this the same in an academy trust? In the best academy trusts school leaders are heavily supported and not left on their own. However, even with this support, living up to all that is expected from a headteacher is a daunting task. It is daunting because of the level of responsibility. Teachers should only take on this role if it excites them. Headteachers will always be subject to high levels of stress, and it is not for everyone. No one should be subjected to unreasonable levels of stress, but, if you want a stress-free life, it's probably not a good idea to become a headteacher, particularly in a school requiring significant improvement.

School leaders will struggle with distinct challenges at different times. An early challenge is establishing credibility (particularly when staff are watching to see whether the new head can hack it). Another is standing up to challenges from children, parents, and even staff colleagues. A strong and supportive deputy head is a godsend at the early stage of headship. When a new head and an established deputy head are not on the same page, however, this can create tension and make the new head's job intensely lonely. These are important moments for a new leader and decisions made in the early days will have significant ramifications down the line. It is a brave head who decides early on to reshape the school's leadership team, but it is a decision that heads into their second and third headships are much more ready to take, as they know how much time this will save in the length of the school's improvement journey. Making such decisions without the support of other school leaders is difficult and risky. School leaders need confidantes outside the school with whom they can discuss such issues.

A school leader gets passed all the trickiest issues that other members of staff have been unable to address successfully. These include complaints from parents. The way school leaders go about addressing parental complaints says a lot about what matters most to them. The natural inclination of almost all school leaders will be to support their staff colleagues and protect them from unreasonable and unfair criticism from parents. It is, however, a foolish school leader who fails to investigate complaints and assumes that every member of staff is perfect.

Realising that a member of staff has erred in the way that a parent alleges is one thing, dealing with it is quite another. The temptation to make the issue go away is strong for all school leaders particularly for those who are new in post. At this point school leaders need to refer to whatever is their 'north star'. Our school system needs headteachers who in this situation keep at the front of their minds the kind of school they wish to lead. Addressing the issue with a member of staff and being prepared to apologise to parents set a tone. It says that in this school we do the right things, not just the easy ones, and we treat everyone properly. Taking such a stance can be extremely lonely.

Some school leaders will find their governors or trustees to be hugely supportive. For others, governors or trustees pushing them in a direction they find uncomfortable can be a very serious reason for feelings of isolation and stress. In these difficult circumstances it is important to establish a working relationship with governors or trustees whereby even in times of differing opinions it is possible to say that the school leader is finding the relationship stressful. Both 'sides' need to find ways of voicing differing opinions while maintaining mutual respect and seeking opportunities to look for common ground.

Ideally, headteachers working in an academy trust should have line managers who are supportive – even when there are challenges – and who provide safe spaces to discuss how that headteacher is feeling. All academy headteachers will face some stress. Poor academy trusts often do not do enough to recognise the pressures they place on headteachers. Headteachers should be among a trust's greatest assets. Academy trust leaders bear the responsibility for knowing how to get the very best from their headteachers and give them the rights levels of both challenge and support. These levels will be different for every headteacher.

Those who hate sport should ignore the next paragraph. Leaders of successful sports teams approaching the end of their season and still in with a chance of winning a trophy are on the edge. Football manager Alex Fergusson famously called this period 'squeaky bum time' – a reference to shifting uncomfortably on a plastic seat towards the end of a tight game – such is the level of tension, expectation, and pressure. School leaders who see tangible progress in their school but still have days when they hold their head in their hands understand this level of tension. Like the most successful football managers, school leaders need to embrace the loneliness, opportunity, and expectations if they are to achieve the outcomes they crave.

A final reason school leadership can be a lonely business is that it is the headteacher's role to protect the school by taking flak for the school's failings, while attributing its successes to the staff by praising others. A reptile park in Australia is responsible for extracting droplets from snakes that become the anti-venom that is available in hospitals. When an unfortunate individual is bitten by a snake and rushed to hospital, they will be given a life-saving anti-venom. Typically, there is much gratitude towards the medical staff, but little recognition of the crucial role played by the donating snake. School leadership can feel a bit similar. Headteachers get all the blame when things go wrong, but when results rise it is the classroom staff who get the praise.

ASIDE

If the worst should happen

In a long career, school leaders may suffer mishaps. These should not prove to be terminal to their career.

There will be times when the challenge of a particular school improvement journey is too much for a specific individual. They may have been dealt an impossible hand, or they may be the wrong person for that project. Whatever the circumstances, sometimes new blood is needed to have any chance of succeeding.

Where possible, school leaders can influence the way they leave a role.

1. Have an experienced negotiator, generally from your trade union, work on your behalf with your employer on the terms of leaving.
2. Push hard on what you want said in an announcement about your departure.
3. Move on quickly – your departure might make it difficult to get a comparable job immediately so be prepared to take on an interim role or a post one layer lower than the one you've left.
4. Get help so that you address the emotional impact and are supported to regain your confidence.
5. Learn from the experience – what might you do differently, but also what kind of organisation would you like to work for next, and what are red flags for organisations to avoid in the future?

MARGINALS

'Marginal gains' – looking for small percentage improvements across every area of activity on the principal that these cumulatively add up to a much greater advantage – is a term coined by Dave Brailsford, former director of British Cycling. The UK cycling team looked for improvements in their own performance, but also in their equipment, preparation, rest, and any other factor they could think of that might feasibly make the slightest difference to their performance. What motivated this determination to find every possible improvement was a drive for excellence. This mindset is exactly the approach needed by school leaders. They should be restless for improvement, and determined not to accept mediocrity, however embedded this may be in some aspects of a school's life.

One of the lessons from the UK cycling team was how they documented and stored data on the improvements they made. They tried out potential improvements, measured if they made a difference, and on that basis decided on whether to keep them or not. School leaders need to be brave enough to try different approaches but also remain open minded enough to ditch an approach that isn't working.

A school leader needs to be outrageously optimistic and thoroughly pragmatic at the same time. A school leader needs to think big and convey the message that everything should be possible for the children in their school. Some school leaders are nervous about talking up the possibilities too high, for fear of being exposed when these great heights are not reached. However, a leader who does not aim high will not achieve heights. Setting ambition high gives at least the possibility of great achievements. Some school leaders thrive on slogans such as 'breaking through the glass ceiling'; they help remind everyone not to settle for mediocrity or to be happy with the status quo. Maintaining such an attitude can be exhausting. A key task of the school leader is to keep up the momentum of school improvement, week after week after week.

Marginal gains can come from external reviews. Reviews often give overall judgments about the extent of progress a school has made from a previous milestone or inspection, but more important are the details of where further improvements can be made. These recommended actions will often be nuanced. They will be important tweaks that finesse the strategies already being implemented and maximise the gains that a school will see from that work. The best external reviewers judge carefully how much a school is ready to take on in terms of the next steps.

Marginal gains can come from strong governance. As with external reviews, those responsible for governance will want to have periodic overall assessments of a school's progress. Even when progress is pleasingly positive, their job is to keep nudging school leaders to look closer at the details and to pay attention to getting them right. The best governance does this in a way that school leaders find not only acceptable but useful.

Ideally, school leaders are confident that those responsible for governance want nothing other than the very best for the school and to help them to be thoroughly successful. Further, given that most school governors have not been school leaders themselves, they need to set up mechanisms to receive the appropriate advice and guidance that allows them to identify the kind of nudges to school practice that will make the most difference. You do not need to have experience of school leadership to be excellent in your role in governance, but you do need to know who to trust to give you guidance.

Another chapter describes the value of visits to other schools, and the benefits certainly include marginal gains. Thoughtful leaders will be selective with what to apply to their own school. They will also work hard to encourage their colleagues to take time to visit other schools and bring back what they have learned. Where schools identify helpful details, it is very useful to feed this information back to the original source. The school that was visited may well be surprised by what has been picked up on. Sometimes the useful detail may be an assumption the school makes, or part of the culture, rather than a specific strategy or action that it has worked on. For example, the school being visited may be particularly proud of the way it supports teachers in the same year groups to do joint planning, but what the school that visited most picked up was that PPA time was half an hour longer a week than in their own school. Consciously identifying best practice in this kind of way can help schools iterate and refine their implementation.

The year-on-year announcement of a school's results for children in year 6, 11, and 13 is a crucial marker in schools' improvement journeys. The pleasure of improved results quickly gives way to the pressure to maintain these, and, if possible, better them further in the following year. All schools acknowledge the variability of different cohorts of children. Success is a positive experience but unfortunately it does not guarantee similar results in future years.

Some aspects of a school's work can build on tried and tested strategies from previous years, but for ambitious schools looking for marginal gains is particularly important. These gains can be about making the best of the available time, understanding the assessment process and format to maximise the marks achieved, and ensuring children are in their very best frame of mind to utilise the learning time in every lesson across the entire year.

A particularly tricky area in looking for marginal gains is the annual performance management cycle that, amongst other purposes, sets each member of staff's salary for the following year. A dilemma arises if a particularly valued and hard-working member of staff has narrowly failed to achieve a previously agreed increase in children's results that has been set out as an objective. Will the school's improvement journey be better supported by giving this member of staff a pay increase or not? To agree to the increase (despite the objective) could appear to lack rigour and determination to make more rapid progress in the school's improvement journey. To decide against the pay rise may be deeply disappointing and appear to lack any recognition of the value of this member of staff. They may even question staying at this school. The school leader needs to think carefully.

Excellence requires a school leader to step back, make demands of themselves, and welcome demands from others. School leaders need to ask themselves how much they want to improve and how much pain and criticism they are prepared to accept in order to achieve that personal growth and development. Some trusts now provide senior leaders, particularly headteachers, the offer of an independent coach to help them with their personal growth and development. The best headteachers approach their own development with the same seriousness as elite athletes. They know that to be at their best requires not only hard work but care in bringing the right mindset and appropriate skills to each tricky situation.

ASIDE

Self-confidence

School leaders are often bedevilled by a lack of self-confidence and self-esteem. Most, however, have extensive experience of supporting children and staff with developing *their* self-confidence and self-esteem. The best organisations will support, encourage, and develop school leaders, but not all will receive such support. For those who do not:

- Believe in yourself — if you don't, why should anyone else?
- Always be courteous to those senior to you but also decide when to ignore their advice — they might be wrong.
- If you keep paper records, anything you've not got to after a month probably can be ignored.
- Don't be chained to emails — if you reply too quickly, you'll only get another one that needs another reply. Decide when you will address emails and limit yourself to those times.
- Remind yourself that you are in charge.
- Work out what is mandatory and what is just advice; even if it is communicated as if it's mandatory.
- Take care asking for legal advice — you will get the most cautious option possible.

NEVER-ENDING

School improvement is a never-ending journey. It has occasional moments of complete fulfilment, but many more with frustrations and temptations to quit. The challenge when the journey seems tough is to focus on the children in the school right now. The school might be great in three years' time – but right now it also needs to be all it possibly can be for the children currently here. This chapter is for everyone involved in school improvement but particularly for those who oversee the system, who are not responsible day-to-day, but rather ensure that the right team is in place.

There can appear to be school leaders who are particularly suitable for turnaround challenges, who are the right people to help a school pull itself up by its bootstraps, when it is really down in the doldrums. Some leaders can oversee a school through this most important of all journeys from being judged thoroughly inadequate to being a good school. Generally, a school has been good for some while before the inspection that validates this change takes place, but what a feeling when that previous failure is finally consigned to the past!

But what is next for such a school? Can the same strategies that took the school from inadequate to good be used for the school's next stage of its improvement journey? There are other school leaders who have the determination for excellence and ability to lead a school to being judged outstanding at inspection.

Some have coined the phrase 'tighten to get good, loosen to get outstanding' but this is not always a recipe for success. Are some school leaders more suited to one part of the school improvement journey than another? Should the system be better at moving successful heads to where they are most needed, or are heads best left to decide where they are best suited (as now)? One of the frustrations of school improvement is that it is far from linear. A highly successful term can be followed by the feeling of two steps forward, three steps backwards. Sometimes it is only in hindsight that the reasons for this bumpy ride can be seen.

System leaders – for example when local authorities had directors of education or the current leaders of multi-academy trusts – need mechanisms to keep abreast of the bumps in the journey in different schools. They need to be nimble, rather than waiting for Ofsted to announce that a school has a problem. The Chief Executive of Camden Council set herself the ambition that local quality assurance would be strong enough that Ofsted was unnecessary. When, for the first time in several years, a primary school was judged inadequate, she was as annoyed that it forced her to recognise that Ofsted was still necessary – even in Camden – as the judgement itself!

Progress in school improvement is non-linear and also not assured. As the academy system matures, we see even the very best trusts in the country find that there are some schools where they do not have success in inspections. They have tried and tested processes and systems, but they still require expert leaders who can effectively implement them, as well as provide the leadership that a particular group of staff needs. Tried and tested processes and systems undoubtedly accelerate school improvement, and as trusts codify their practices there is a growing understanding of how to replicate them across schools. However, the age-old requirement for headteachers who can lead people, inspire communities, and provide compassionate and effective behaviour management remains as crucial as ever.

Let's look through the inspection history of a school in Reading. This school was judged inadequate but subsequently improved and was assessed as good through a couple of inspection cycles. Then the story changed. Although the school had the same headteacher and the same chair of governors who had helped it improve, it still went back to being judged inadequate. In response it joined an academy trust and refreshed leadership, and its next inspection report read much better, with the school back to being judged good. Those who oversee groups of schools yearn for the consistency of reputation and success that the best schools in the country – both publicly funded and independent – enjoy. The all too common roller-coaster of success and failure is not good enough. School leaders should not need Ofsted to tell them their job.

Trusts have developed tried and tested processes and systems for school improvement as well as monitoring and evaluating progress in each school for which they are responsible. This is likely to include performance management arrangements, where school leaders will have demanding expectations and targets to meet. Thoughtful trusts are conscious of the impact of these expectations and targets on school leaders and their colleagues. Trust leaders must tread a careful line between holding firm to very high expectations while being realistic and humane about their toll on a trust's most important assets, its headteachers. The trust that gets this right will succeed over the long term even if it will sometimes have to bear the frustration or feeling more like the tortoise than the hare.

Why is school improvement never-ending? Why is it so hard? In the end, children may be hard work, but they are only one of the challenges, and schools are full of people who are talented and skilled working with children. Similarly, while in some schools relationships with parents go awry and putting this right is not straightforward, there *are* strategies that work well. Furthermore, once a school has good processes for dealing with parents then those same parents have the capacity to provide additional support in helping their children make good progress. The biggest challenge in school improvement is to get *all* staff singing from the same song sheet at the same quality as the very *best* member of staff. No school can be an effective school without an effective head teacher. A headteacher cannot make a school good on their own, but they can undermine the efforts of many good staff if they lack the skills needed for school improvement. An effective school also needs an effective teacher in every classroom. To get every teacher to be effective requires not just the headteacher but every other senior leader to coach, cajole, and encourage their colleagues.

Once all this is in place, there are still rabbit holes that can seriously impede the school improvement journey. One of the most obvious is the school reception. If you want to start to understand the difference school receptions make, try phoning a school and asking to speak to their headteacher. Their response will tell you much about the culture of the school and the extent to which even an oft-stated commitment to respect is lived out in practice.

It's like painting the Forth Road Bridge – by the time you reach one end you have to start over – there are always aspects of school life that need attention and improvement. Often these include parts that a school leader thought had been sorted and yet now once more require further attention.

ASIDE

Aspirations

What are your medium and long term aspirations for your career and your school?

Where do you expect to be in five or ten years' time?

Where would you like to be in five or ten years' time?

It won't happen unless you make it happen.

OFSTED

Ofsted is Ofsted. No manual can explain how to get a better inspection judgement than the school deserves. Indeed, no manual should try to do so. To do well in an Ofsted inspection, be a good school. This is of course no easy feat and can only be achieved through years of dedicated work.

Ofsted inspections can be feared or loved. The actual experience of inspection varies. A bad result is generally very difficult to take but these rare occasions are greatly outnumbered by the inspections which school leaders find positive and validating. Much worse than the inspection experience itself is the wait and anticipation. This was particularly bad in the immediate post-covid period when Ofsted lengthened the gap that they considered reasonable between inspections.

Some of the very best people in education have gone into inspection. The most skilled inspectors can explain even very critical judgments in ways that are not only acceptable to school leaders but that lead to positive school improvement. Less experienced inspectors can come across as more reserved, less willing to explain how their thinking is evolving during the inspection, and twitchier when challenged. School leaders work hard at building a relationship with inspectors. Some inspectors respond so well that the experience is a positive one, regardless of the outcome.

Some school leaders, particularly trust leaders, decide to combatively take on inspectors, challenge every comment they don't like, and suggest that inspectors will have to have unbelievably good evidence to challenge the school leaders' own assessment and suggestions. My personal opinion is that this is entirely inappropriate and comes close to deliberately distorting both the inspection process and its eventual judgement.

Whether a school comes out of an inspection with the judgement it hopes for is mostly dependent on the success of its work in the preceding years. However, just as no student should go into a public examination anything other than thoroughly prepared, no sensible school should go into an inspection without being ready. School leaders know from their experience of recruitment the importance of initial impressions when they are making selections. They should not underestimate the importance of the initial phone call with the lead inspector. Of course, they will be well-prepared for questions about the quality of education, but even more important is the tone and attitude that the headteacher conveys during this conversation.

Two key areas that some school leaders find hard during inspection are *listening* and *providing evidence* that inspectors need. There will be times during the inspection when the school leader finds it difficult to understand how a reasonable inspector could possibly come to the kind of conclusions that are being suggested. The best advice at these times is to listen. The odder the conclusion the inspector appears to be reaching, the more urgently you need to understand how they could have come to such a view based on what has been seen so far.

Another critical piece of advice is to keep providing evidence. Inspectors conduct a remarkable amount of observations and conversations but cannot possibly see everything that happens within school. They will look to see enough to have confidence in the judgements they are coming to. Where school leaders believe that a different judgment would be a fairer assessment, they will need to find evidence and provide it in easily digestible forms. For example, if the evidence an inspector needs to see is contained in a huge arch lever file of minutes of trustee meetings, then they will need a quick guide and markers to show particular pages that have key information. If inspectors query a school leader's assessment, that school leader needs to provide succinct example data with a straightforward analysis and explanation of the conclusions that the school leader believes are justified.

Is there a value in training as an inspector if you are a school leader? There are few more valuable professional development opportunities. However, both the training itself, and the time taken each term in inspections, require a significant commitment. In return, not only does a school leader get a detailed understanding of the framework for inspection, but the inspections themselves are deeply rewarding. It is a privilege to get to know a school in such detail in just two days. Participating in team meetings and wrestling over the appropriate judgment for a school brings home to a school leader the importance of complete school improvement and not just cosmetic short-term boosts.

As a school leader there will come a time when your school is 'in the Ofsted window'. Each Monday to Wednesday lunchtime you will be left wondering if this is the week. Within a trust, this means having a contingency plan for how the diary will be amended if there is a call to one of the trust schools on a Monday morning. One challenge is to keep improving while waiting. There is nothing more disappointing than feeling we were better prepared last term than this one. Another challenge is that no matter how much the matter preys on your mind, don't allow this pressure to filter right across the school. The rest of the school needs to be well-prepared but also feel confident that, when the time comes, the plan will come out of the drawer, and the school will have an excellent couple of days.

A common discussion point on the afternoon prior to the inspection – while preparing and providing documentation for the inspection team – is whether to tell the inspectors what grades the school would self-assess itself as. There are some inspectors who, if they are not given a school's self-evaluation, will challenge school leaders over the strength of their understanding of their own school. When school leaders decide not to include grades – or whatever form of self-evaluation they provide – they need to be clear and explicit that they believe the decision about grades is one for an inspector. In general, when school leaders are looking to push for the higher of two grades, they include a self-evaluation. Often, not including a self-evaluation indicates a nervousness about 'giving it away', i.e. helping an inspector tell the school a difficult message.

Could Ofsted itself improve? Too right it could! My top ten suggestions are:

1. Listening and collaboration should be the hallmarks of the system.
2. School heads and deputies should be encouraged to move into HMI roles through secondments so that there is a greater understanding of school leadership across the organisation.

3. The top concerns in schools – at the time of writing, these would include pupil attendance and supporting children with special educational needs – should be inspected with sympathy and a view to identifying best practices to share across the system.

4. Inspection of safeguarding should be against a grade rather than having binary 'cliff-edge' consequences.

5. Schools should be told the school year that they can expect to be inspected in advance (as already happens with diocesan inspections).

6. The terrible gap in activity following an inadequate judgement should be reduced so that schools and their leaders have support in place no more than four weeks after an inspection.

7. Achieving consistency in inspection is about the behaviour of inspectors rather than fundamentalist adherence to each phrase of the framework.

8. The quality of reports needs to improve through increased detail.

9. Ofsted should use its work and expertise across children's services to contribute to thinking and discussions about how to support success for the most challenged children.

10. Ofsted should develop closer institutional relationships with the research world so that the huge amount of data and insights gathered by Ofsted can be used by others for analysis and research.

ASIDE

Quote bingo

Match the Ofsted Chief Inspectors Chris Woodhead, Mike Tomlinson, David Bell, Christine Gilbert, Michael Wilshaw, and Amanda Spielman to these quotations.

1. 'Not all teachers are professional, not all teachers are committed, not all teachers do their best, and it's the job of a headteacher to identify the great majority who do their best and those who don't'.

2. 'It is no longer enough for schools to be "satisfactory"'.

3. 'A "culture of fear" exists around England's school inspections'.

4. 'If you're the chief inspector, you should always see it as your first responsibility to defend the interests of learners, wherever they're being educated'.

5. '15,000 teachers are incompetent and should be sacked'.

6. 'I don't give a monkey's toss for them [teachers], all I care about is the children'.

Answers: 1. Michael Wilshaw 2. Christine Gilbert 3. Amanda Spielman 4. David Bell 5. Chris Woodhead 6. Mike Tomlinson

PARENTS

All staff in schools need to be accomplished at communicating with parents. School leaders have a particular responsibility to model how to do this in a way that is not defensive or patronising and treats parents with respect. School leaders need to develop regular routines around the communications that parents need. They should not underestimate the reassurance it gives parents to know when and where events take place and the routines their children will have across each week or even day.

School leaders should also not underestimate the anxiety caused when simple scheduling matters such as the day children should bring their PE kit are changed without notice. They should set the tone by showing parents that they know that these things matter. As well as the routines of school life, school leaders will want to engage parents with the learning that their children will undertake at school. The effective organisation of the school is significantly enhanced when parents understand the routines and expectations they and their children must fulfil. Most importantly, a child's learning is accelerated when there is an effective partnership between the school and their parents. For example, this may be the most important factor in early reading development, where having regular time every day reading with an adult at home as well as at school makes a big difference.

There is a risk that poorly implemented attempts to develop links with parents appear as pushing responsibility for children's learning onto parents. Particularly weak examples of this are where schools send home vague instructions for 'projects' parents should do with their children. There will of course be parents who will follow this up and give significant help to their children – in turn those children will benefit from this learning. This strategy, however, simply reinforces the advantages that children with highly competent parents, or those who are engaged and have time, already have. The job of schools is to support *all* children. If a particular project is worth doing, school leaders need to find ways for every child to tackle it. Where parents can add value to this, all well and good, but such projects need to be undertaken in a way that is not dependent on parental input.

School leaders should beware acronyms and euphemisms when communicating with parents (or the public generally) – for example, 'Next Friday is a Baker Day' could mean many things to a parent new to bringing their child to school. If parents are left to guess, then the idea that they will have to arrange childcare that day might be far from their mind. School leaders need to develop formats for the way that they communicate with parents so that key information can quickly be retrieved and understood.

The most successful communicators will develop a style that moves beyond just giving information and engages parents with what it is that the school is attempting to achieve. When school leaders succeed with establishing a style that parents actually want to read, they have the opportunity not just to state the school's values but to explain and exemplify them. The aim of establishing a style for communications is to engage parents as co-educators. Where possible, school leaders need to avoid careless jargon creeping into school vocabulary, for example, in our school 'the packed lunch Goldfish' are the children in the class we call Goldfish who currently bring a packed lunch to school. A reference like this will be entirely meaningless and possibly bizarre to parents.

A particular challenge is communication when something difficult has happened in the school. The rule of thumb is to communicate quickly and fully. The aim is to be up front and to give confidence to parents that, no matter how difficult the issue which has arisen, the school's leadership is on top of the matter and knows how to address it. An exception to this will be when other agencies are involved; if the police are involved then there may be restrictions on what can be said publicly. When police are involved, a school will need professional support from either the local authority, or trust PR lead (who will have links with press offices of other agencies), and quickly agree the extent to which public comment is possible and advisable. With serious challenges, for example after a poor inspection judgement, writing a letter to parents is not enough and parents should be offered the opportunity to meet with the school leader.

Open meetings are fraught with challenges. When successfully handled, they can help parents continue to have confidence in the school leadership despite whatever public criticisms there may have been. However, such meetings run the risk of being dominated by strongly critical parents and end up further reducing school leaders' credibility.

The way a school leader addresses complaints says a lot about the way they live out their values. All school leaders will claim their values include high levels of respect for all connected with the school including parents. This can be tested by the response to complaints. When a parent makes a complaint, it may or may not be justified. The serious school leader will make no assumptions, treat the complainant with respect and consider the possibility that they have a justification. If it turns out that the complaint does have merit, the integrity of the school leader is shown by their response. In general, this response should start with, 'I would like to apologise for …'. In many cases this will diffuse the matter and reassure the parents that their concern has been taken seriously and is being addressed.

School leaders will also receive complaints that are not justified, and the school leader is not able to uphold the concern that a parent has put forward. Communicating this to a parent again needs to be courteous, understanding, and clear. In a small number of cases, a parent will choose to take the complaint to whatever further stages the school's complaints process allows. All communication needs to be written in a way that considers not only the needs of the parents but also how it might later be reviewed by a complaints panel looking at how well the school dealt with this case.

In recent years, school leaders have had to cope with comments, remarks, and complaints that are not sent directly to the school but are made very publicly through the various social media platforms. Some school leaders find this very challenging. The best advice is not to read it and only to respond to communication that is sent to the school. Some school leaders get very concerned about comments on social media that are downright untrue and sometimes feel that it is essential to put the record straight. Understandable as this is, it is generally unwise. Once this has begun then each fresh distortion of the truth will also need to be challenged. None of us like reading negative comments about ourselves but there are two principles that school leaders need to hang onto. The first of these is that today's news is forgotten tomorrow, and the second is that responding to a comment in general draws it to far wider attention.

Nothing beats the relationships developed with parents by school leaders by being consistently and routinely on the school gate. This is particularly effective in primary schools. It enables relationships to be built that enhance the culture and ambience at the school, but also develops social capital needed for the tricky moments when parents are finding things difficult about the school. In secondary schools being on the gate is more about greeting the students. School leaders need to find ways of 'appearing on the gate' (literally and metaphorically) in whatever school it is they are leading and whatever age the students are, for example by having a high profile at every event at which parents come into the school.

ASIDE

Ofsted Parentview – views of parents

Parents agree or strongly agree:

My child is happy at this school	89%
My child feels safe at this school	90%
The school makes sure its pupils are well behaved	83%
The school makes me aware of what my child will learn during the year	80%
My child has SEN, and the school gives them the support they need to succeed	67%
The school has high expectations for my child	82%
My child does well at this school	87%
The school lets me know how my child is doing	83%
There is a good range of subjects available to my child at this school	91%
My child can take part in clubs and activities at this school	90%
The school supports my child's wider personal development	78%
I would recommend this school to another parent	84%

QUARTERMASTER

Many of the chapters of this book are about school leaders, generally headteachers or sometimes trust leaders. School improvement, however, requires more than just leaders. In the military world, alongside the battle tactics and strategy, an army requires significant energy, logistics, and resources, and this is the job of the quartermaster. Analogous figures exist outside of the military, Margaret Thatcher credited her ministerial colleague William Whitelaw for the support he provided ('Everyone needs a Willy'). A more light-hearted reference point would be 'Q', the genius of logistics and gadgets from the James Bond movies. How brave a school leader would be to appoint their own 'Q' to a school leadership team to bring some panache to school improvement!

In the school improvement world, wise leaders will identify or appoint a 'quartermaster' to do the grunt work that is required day in, day out to make things work. In some schools this key role is carried out by someone not traditionally on the leadership team, who has not come through the roles of a teacher, middle leader, and senior leader. In some cases, they are called a 'school bursar' or 'operations manager'. In some schools – perhaps particularly as part of trusts – the role is played by someone who is part of the trust's central team rather than on the school's own. And then in yet other schools the role is one of the school's senior leaders, perhaps most typically an experienced deputy head. Whatever their role is titled, and wherever it appears in the hierarchy, these individuals are indispensable and valued like gold dust by their headteachers – they need to be fixers, excellent organisers, and generally completely unflappable.

The kind of work that they do can cover almost every area of school life. A skilful headteacher makes particular use of such colleagues when the abilities they offer come less naturally to the headteacher. There is likely to be communication and conversations many times each day between the headteacher and this valuable member of staff. These individuals need to be skilled, knowledgeable, and crucially on the same wavelength as the headteacher. Such an understanding means that other colleagues across the school can talk with this member of staff as if they were the headteacher and this can be a particularly important tactic in accelerating the pace of school improvement. It avoids the inhibiting factor of everything needing to go through the headteacher, whose time is finite.

These highly trusted, reliable, senior colleagues, have the potential to significantly accelerate the school improvement journey, but they can also become blockers or real obstacles. Headteachers – however close their relationship with such key colleagues – have a responsibility to maintain a distance that allows them to see when a member of staff they previously considered indispensable is finding it hard to continue. The headteacher needs to be able to have frank conversations with this most trusted member of staff, even if they have also become a close professional friend. The headteacher also needs to avoid the risk of jealousy if they are perceived by senior staff as having a much stronger relationship with one individual.

Let's look at desirable attributes for a number of other school leadership positions. First up, what makes a great deputy head? The deputy head has two key roles. The first is to cover all of the disparate areas identified in their – most probably over-long – job description. This is already a big job, but in fulfilling it they should also model responsibility and best practice for the rest of the staff. Their second job is easier to explain but even more important. They should assist the headteacher in being the best that they can be. This support role is not easy and will look different in practice with every headteacher. It requires listening and communication and works best when both the headteacher and deputy head are prepared to work out an effective personal and professional relationship and are able to openly discuss what works well and what is difficult between them.

Next, what makes a great early years leader? There are some obvious pitfalls to avoid when selecting early years leaders. Early years leaders with great promise and strong practice can waste these if they focus their energies on keeping early years teaching as an oasis separate from the rest of the school. Similarly, avoid early years leaders who behave as if they are the only member of staff who understands very young children. Good early years leaders understand children, have high ambitions for what those children can achieve, and how adults can help young children realise that potential. Great early years leaders bring this understanding and experience to the whole school, helping their colleagues understand how young children learn and how adults can make a difference in the progress of that learning.

What makes a great head of sixth form? Many staff think this would be a dream job, but don't be fooled, it is unbelievably demanding to do it effectively. There will be many demands on your time and many people who have strong opinions about what you should be doing. You will have to make sure that young people want to come to the sixth form. You will have to make sure that those young people who do come to the sixth form enjoy it. And – despite the fact that your teaching role will be only a small part of the sixth form offer – you will have to make sure that those young people achieve excellent results. In amongst all of this, a key part of your role is staff management. Although many staff enjoy sixth form teaching, a good head of sixth form ensures that all staff push the boat out and give as much effort to each lesson as they do with the most demanding classes in younger year groups. Great heads of sixth form do not just confine themselves to sixth form work. They also understand how a strong sixth form provides role models of exemplary young people that can significantly and positively affect the whole culture of the school.

Finally, what makes a great SENCO? A strong SENCO, of course, needs to be highly knowledgeable about children with special educational needs and the legal framework within which schools operate, as well as having a passion for helping children with special educational needs succeed. A great SENCO will also be determined to have an impact right across the school. They will not just expect adaptations to specific lessons to meet a particular child's needs, they will look to make practice across the school inclusive of the needs of all children.

A great SENCO will not only change practice but transform the culture of the school from simply coping with children with differences to welcoming and embracing the diversity they bring. School leaders have a great responsibility towards SENCOs. The changes that SENCOs need staff to embrace are often challenging. This requires the explicit backing of the headteacher and needs to be regularly reinforced and followed up.

Going back to 'Q' – there are gadgets that can accelerate school improvement and those that slow it down. In strong schools, effective use of IT can significantly support children's learning. In weak schools, a focus on IT is likely to be a diversion that reduces the pace of improvement. The gadgets that school leaders most need are those that keep focus on the big areas where the school needs to improve.

ASIDE

Perverse incentives

The DfE faces the constant challenge of how to incentivise school improvement while avoiding perverse incentives. For example, a tricky area has been Key Stage 1 (KS1) performance. Up until 2023 KS1 performance was used as the baseline for the Key Stage 2 progress measure – meaning that the lower that the KS1 performance measure was assessed as being then the higher the KS2 progress measure would likely be. A further example in recent times is the funding available for trusts taking on schools in problem areas identified by the DfE, which encourages trusts to consider taking on schools in those areas. This is all well and good until outlying schools in areas not yet attracting funding get ignored.

Trusts now can allocate funding as they see best and face similar challenges in incentivising the behaviours they most want to see. Questions they have to confront include:

- Is an experienced teacher 'worth' more from a financial perspective than a brand new teacher just out of training?
- Should in-year deficits be cumulative as in the past or should each year be treated afresh?
- 'Integrated curriculum financial planning' focuses on efficient leadership and staffing teams but assumes equal skill from equally paid staff.
- How is capital funding best allocated? By overall trust assessments of need or via bidding?
- Is money better spent on new windows or improving libraries?

RESILIENCE

School improvement journeys always have bumps and difficulties along the way. For school leaders to be successful they need to be able to withstand and bounce back from the challenges these difficulties present. The term resilience might have been made for school leaders embarking on school improvement.

The term resilience is also used to describe animals who can adapt to or survive sudden and sometimes traumatic change. Although the resilient school leader may not navigate and negotiate the difficulties that occur any better than others, they will be less scarred by them and more ready to face whatever comes next. They learn and develop the toughness – whatever the knocks – to adapt, survive, and thrive.

Resilience comes more naturally to some of us than others. No one has a monopoly on resilience or can guarantee that nothing will ever knock them. However, some school leaders are more naturally disposed to riding the ups and downs of school improvement. Wherever a school leader is in that spectrum, all can develop strategies and ways of working that prepare them to better manage the situations they find difficult. When handling tricky and difficult situations, headteachers need to remind themselves that the hardest issues always come their way – if an issue is straightforward, it is unlikely to reach the headteacher.

When staff need to make difficult decisions, they may well look to the headteacher for validation. However, those same staff may well not take kindly to the decision itself being challenged. The responsibility for dealing with the trickiest issues is why headteachers are the highest paid in every school. A particular challenge for new headteachers preparing for their first role is the realisation of how little they actually know about the job despite having been absolutely certain they were up to carrying it out.

Some of the issues school leaders have to address will be extremely emotionally demanding for all concerned. The school leader will not only have to support all involved but may well be struggling themselves. At these times – which may well be uncharted territory for a new school leader – it is essential that they also have emotional support and are not dealing with these difficulties on their own.

Those responsible for overseeing schools, particularly academy trusts, have a responsibility to put in place advice and support for school leaders. This should include emotional support for those bearing the brunt of the most difficult issues. School leaders themselves also need to take responsibility for ensuring that they have the necessary support at difficult times. The system needs to help school leaders to withstand the pressures such events can bring. After all, being over-stressed is unhelpful in keeping a cool head and making well-balanced responses in times of crisis.

In some difficult situations, the cold hard truth is that the school has messed up. A school leader needs to have the ability to front up and accept when the school has been poorer than parents have the right to expect. This is not easy, and criticism can be bruising. These are times when the school leader has to take one for the team … whether or not they were personally responsible for whatever has gone wrong. Headteachers need to remember that they run the school. If one of their staff messes up, it is the head who has put them in that role, and so bears ultimate responsibility. Taking responsibility is one thing, being thoroughly mortified is another. Being thoroughly mortified is no good to anyone if you are indecisive and inactive as a result. The resilient school leader fronts up to errors and failures but moves on quickly to proactively putting things right.

A potentially debilitating area of a school leader's work is dealing with complaints. Wherever possible, school leaders need to hear concerns and respond to them. When a complaint is upheld, school leaders need to accept responsibility and put things right. In many, many cases treating parents with respect and listening carefully to their concerns will be sufficient to deal with complaints. However, there will also be some occasions when parents use the full range of the complaints procedure. For headteachers encountering this situation for the first time, this is very demanding. There are a number of principles for dealing with complaints:

- Follow the complaints procedure to the letter.
- The subject of a complaint cannot be the one to address the issue. When a complaint concerns the headteacher then someone from beyond the school's leadership needs to be involved – generally this will be a chair of governors, but in a trust it can be someone else.
- Although in general responding rapidly shows an appropriate level of courtesy, there will be times when it is more judicious to slow things down and reply in a much more measured timescale. This can take the sting out of criticisms that are stated in robust or even unpleasant language.

Support mechanisms for school leaders need to be in place well before any crisis arises. A common problem for school leaders is that they may not have invested enough time and energy into relationships that could provide support before a crisis hits and they find themselves struggling to cope. Support mechanisms should include a senior staff team that operates as a group within which responses to crisis situations are batted around and improved before being finalised. Governors and trustees are not there to pick up the pieces when operational matters go wrong, but they can provide invaluable support when school leaders most need it, as long they stay up to date with their leaders' most pressing concerns. Providing appropriate support mechanisms for heads is an area where many multi-academy trusts need to improve.

Whatever organisation they work for, school staff should have comprehensive packages of wellbeing support available. While many staff are too reserved to step forward and accept such support, it is important that staff take responsibility for their wellbeing and attendance. School leaders need to model signing in to and using the support systems that their organisations offer. This includes responding to emails at civilised times (an email late in the evening or at the weekend should only be sent in a real emergency) and setting the tone by keeping work within reasonable hours. The school where staff are not regularly in school before 7.30am or after 6pm will find – on the rare occasions when a late evening or whatever uncivilised requirement is needed – that staff are willing to do this. The school that tacitly expects its staff to regularly work all hours will find that they burn out and become resentful.

Some organisations offer their school leaders independent coaching. Where this isn't the case, school leaders might consider paying for this themselves. There is enormous potential value to input from someone with coaching skills – not necessarily from an education background – in helping school leaders with the emotional management of challenging situations. This support can make the difference for heads who feel they are relentlessly dealing with one challenging situation after another.

School leaders need to pay attention to the resilience of all their colleagues as well as themselves. This requires a clarity of expectations, support in meeting those expectations, systems in place to help when staff struggle with work or in their personal lives, and a professionalism that supports people to meet the expectation that they do their jobs properly. The most effective schools have a common culture where it is not just one or two senior leaders who demonstrate resilience, but this is shared widely by many staff. Some schools set out resilience for children as one of their ambitions. Well-run schools provide support for all children, whether or not they come from a family that has already given them confidence and early resilience.

The English school system has always had excellent schools. It has also had two weak characteristics:

- Schools that fluctuate in performance and depend too much on the success or otherwise of their latest headteacher.
- Schools in very disadvantaged areas have often been very poor over decades.

One of the ambitions of the academy trust system should be to strengthen the resilience of the school system so that this volatility of performance is replaced by it being much more predictable. A trust should aim to guarantee continued strong performance across changes of leadership. Each new head should be the guardian of a school's ethos, values, and procedures, rather than being the latest in the line of bright new ideas to relaunch a school. I believe a limited number of trusts are emerging that can break the cycle of entrenched poor performance – the country needs these school leaders to be encouraged to take on yet more of the weakest schools in the country.

ASIDE

Schools' Wellbeing Partnership

In a whole school approach, wellbeing and mental health are everyone's business, with genuine engagement across the entire community: staff, pupils, governors, parents, and external services. This approach involves multiple components including early identification and intervention; staff wellbeing and development; and skills-based work for pupils; but above all it adopts a positive and universal focus on wellbeing.

Why have a whole school approach? Visit the Schools' Wellbeing Partnership website: https://www.schoolswellbeing.org.uk.

We aim to:

- Support schools in implementing a whole school approach to mental health and wellbeing (For the 'whole school approach' visit, https://www. ncb.org.uk/what-we-do/improving-practice/wellbeing-mental-health/ schools-wellbeing-partnership/whole-school).

- Increase awareness of the importance of children and young people's emotional wellbeing and how this connects to learning.

- Inspire education settings to incorporate measures that will improve children and young people's wellbeing.

- Equip teachers, staff, and young people with the skills and knowledge to prioritise and address wellbeing and mental health.

Why this matters:

- Half of lifetime mental illness starts by the age of 14.
- Suicide is one of the leading causes of death for young people.
- In an average classroom, 4 children will have a clinically diagnosed mental health condition, 7 will have been bullied, and 8 will have experienced severe physical violence, sexual abuse, or neglect.
- Early intervention and a whole school approach can be highly effective in improving wellbeing and reducing the impact of mental health problems.

SPECIALISTS

There are often specialists who have knowledge or understandings that can help school leaders and their staff get to grips with important aspects of school improvement work. Specialists will have seen many schools in the same position – in their particular area of their expertise – and know how those schools have made quick and significant changes. When a school makes use of specialists, it is important that they listen carefully to the implementation detail of the programme that is advised. However, there will be times when the bigger picture trumps specialists, and when school leaders know best even though a specialist knows their area. School leaders need to decide when to adhere with complete fidelity to what a specialist is proposing and when there are other elements of the school's priorities that outweigh the specialist's recommendations. These are important judgements.

Schools are likely to identify curriculum specialists so that they are not dependent on their own subject leaders being on top of every possibility. Specialists can advise on curriculum, teaching approaches, assessment, and interventions, but the most valuable specialists, or consultants, are those prepared to work alongside teachers in their classrooms and both model and teach alongside them. Working with this kind of specialist requires teachers to have the right attitude and a willingness to learn and change their practice.

School leaders can sometimes face the strange challenge of being offered too much support, indeed more than teachers have the capacity to absorb. In these cases, school leaders need to be assertive about the curriculum support that can be taken on in any particular term and, where necessary, shift some offered support on to later terms.

There are several forms of financial support that may be needed by a school at different stages of its school improvement journey. For example, a poor school may have had weaknesses in its staff and thus sought to recruit new teachers. While making the changes needed, the school may have to be over-staffed to achieve progress, and a trust will have to decide the extent of additional funding it will allocate to the school. For some trusts this may sound unpalatable. However, experienced trusts know that school improvement requires investment in a number of ways, and this includes financial investment. In a very different way, schools often actually benefit from a very rigorous analysis of their spending, especially if it cuts spending tied to old assumptions that need challenging.

Most trusts now use 'integrated curriculum financial planning' and use benchmarks on spending, particularly on the efficiency of the use of the school's staff. The most effective trusts find sufficient money to fund the specialists which can help accelerate schools' improvement. The third area of financial support every trust should provide, is making savings through scale. This is easy to understand in principle, but in reality never straightforward to achieve.

There can be some savings made by procuring on behalf of several schools at the same time. The most important saving, however, is the efficiency of 'back office' staff, and that the trust's in house finance team, etc., will generally cost less than whoever individual schools used to buy this service from. Trusts have significant responsibilities for school buildings, and significant capital budgets each year to oversee these. A common feature of many schools that join trusts when in trouble is that their buildings have been badly neglected. Addressing this is an important part of each school's overall improvement.

All schools need HR expertise but those at the early stages of a school improvement journey need it even more, and more frequently, than other schools. Trusts need HR teams that understand the changes needed in school teams, and how to make these changes without exposing the trust to any risk. The HR teams also need to be able to deal with everyone humanely, decently, and reasonably, including those who may not be up to staying in their role. School leaders need to be able to share their challenges with their HR colleagues and get constructive advice on how to make things happen, not just why they are not possible. Good HR support should also include how to help school leaders have, rather than avoid, difficult conversations.

One of the strongest advantages of larger trusts is that they can employ specialists with both recognised qualifications and experience in their area. For example, rather than the traditional jack of all trades school bursar a larger trust can have a procurement expert who should make further savings well above the cost of their post. Rather than the stretched capacity that has been the mark of school management – where heads try hard to understand all aspects of the school's business – in a trust a head should spend much less time in areas outside their expertise, allowing those areas to be handled by people who actually know what they are talking about.

Some school leaders rarely ask for legal advice on the grounds they won't like what they hear. Trusts need to engage reliable legal advisers to give them timely advice that enables them to take things forward. School leaders need advice that removes barriers rather than adds to them. However, no sensible school leader will want to make misguided decisions that leads their trust into difficulties. Leaders should listen carefully and pay attention to advice that is useful and helpful, even if it is annoying and unwelcome.

While there is a longer chapter in this book on external reviews, school leaders are reviewing every day. No day should go by without some kind of 'learning walk' around the school, but it should also include a focussed look at some specific children and what progress they are or are not making in a particular area. This will need supplementing from time to time with specialists – not just in specific areas but also in school improvement overall. These specialists are very important in our school system – not only can they see the bigger picture very quickly but they generally do so much more than inspectors. It's one thing to assess how well a school is doing yourself. Advice from a specialist who can put their finger on exactly what the school needs to focus on to move on to the next stages in the school's improvement journey, is worth its weight in gold.

One further area of specialist expertise that is worth understanding is that of civil servants. It is easy for school leaders to initially be a bit dismissive of civil servants, who although bright, engaging, and conscientious, do not have experience or wide understanding of school life. However, it's not their job to have this understanding. It's their job to administer the system in the way that their ministers expect. School leaders do well to understand an expertise that is alien to their own experience and learn to work with civil servants as colleagues in the school improvement journey.

ASIDE

Mathematics

The best specialist mathematics support focuses on the identification, sharing, and transfer of effective practice. Supported by specialists, teachers recognise that classrooms are the laboratory for improvement. Instructional quality can be improved through a process of engaging in supported collaborative enquiry, coaching or lesson study, gathering evidence on what works and why, and identifying what needs to be improved and how.

This works best embedded within whole-school improvement planning, managed, and fully supported by senior leaders.

Secure language and reasoning skills and the use of imagery and symbols are essential features of mathematics learning. Good mathematics teaching requires secure subject knowledge with a clear understanding of curricular progression and of how children learn mathematics. Engaging teachers in mathematics at their own level is an essential element of improving practice.

(It is the privilege of an author to be outrageously opinionated and unchallenged in selecting the most important subject to have specialists.)

TRUSTS

The purpose of an academy trust is to take advantage of trust freedoms to give school leaders the ability to take the actions they see fit to improve schools as quickly as they are able. There's no point in a school being part of an academy trust if this does not contribute to more rapid school improvement.

The majority of academy trusts started with just one school. Most were good or very good schools. In time, however, the favoured version became multi-academy trusts where those with one or more very strong schools were deemed appropriate to take on very weak schools that needed rapid improvement. These trusts were able to draw on the strengths of their successful schools to provide support to the weaker ones. There are many varieties of academy trust in terms of size, of school performance, and of the range of types of school (whether that be by phase, number of children at each school, or the local authority areas that the school serves). Some trusts have also taken up the opportunity, now open only to trusts, to apply to be responsible for opening new schools.

The academy system is still relatively under-developed and an understanding of what makes for successful trusts is still emerging. There are trusts succeeding with different approaches, but elements that make for success are clearly emerging. For example, for a long time, heads in particular were very hung up on whose autonomy was being promoted in the development of a trust. However, the value of consistency has clearly trumped individual teachers setting out their own approaches and expectations in their own classrooms.

The early messaging around academy freedoms was based on the assumption that school leaders knew how to run their school best.

As long as a school ran successfully, then that school should be run with as few restraints as possible. Within just a few years, though, the emphasis shifted subtly to schools being in groups as academies rather than on their own. The unit of accountability has moved from the individual school to the trust. Crucially, these trusts have been constituted from both successful and extremely unsuccessful schools. Generally, the school improvement strategy has been to take the processes, curriculum, and often even specific staff from successful schools and get the weak schools to take on these elements.

Subsequently to this, two developments have made the system more complex. The first of these was that not all trusts had that shining excellent school on which to base their operating model, or in some cases that previously highly thought of school began to do less well. The second was that trusts began to have many more ordinary schools too, neither utterly amazing nor extremely poor. There began to be a much greater variety of approaches with two extremes with many falling somewhere between. At one end of the spectrum, a trust is a club of schools – united by shared resources and possibly back-office staff and administrative functions – where each headteacher continues to decide how their school runs. This version of a trust has an initial attraction to heads who believe that they know best. Many outside the trust will wonder what the point of being in such a trust is. This way of working is fine until one of the schools begins to do less well, and at that stage there is little choice other than to put in a new head with better ideas. At the other end of the spectrum, one single clear operating model for nearly every facet of school life is developed and every school in the trust follows every aspect of this operating model. This is only successful if the operating model is completely sound. If it proves unsuccessful it holds the risk of *all* the schools in that trust coming unstuck.

A third route for the operation of a multi-academy trust is for there to be a shared dialogue about where common ways of working should be introduced and where to be less prescriptive, as there is not yet sufficient evidence of any particular approach being successful. Where there is confidence in specific approaches these can then be codified and set expectations across the trust. The way such decisions are made is crucial. Whichever approach a trust takes, none will be successful without a good head teacher. It is incumbent on a trust not only to recruit excellent head teachers but for these headteachers to be leaders in their own right, who enjoy making decisions about the way their school runs. The key is how a trust helps school leaders have their cake and eat it. Being in a trust should provide school leaders with the very best support and advice about tried and tested ways of working. However, those same leaders should also have been part of the debate about what is considered tried and tested, and what is subsequently codified for all the schools in the trust.

Once a trust decides its approach and where it stands on the extent of codification, and its expectations of fidelity to these approaches, it is important to communicate these conclusions to school leaders. Successful trusts will keep this conversation alive and under regular review and will make sure headteachers are thoroughly involved, rather than handing these decisions down from above.

No organisation likes to feel that there is some remote HQ handing down instructions with little opportunity to have any input. The more schools are involved, the more complex trust structures become. This is likely to include an overall leader, probably called the trust chief executive, and then the trust central team, an intervening group who are the line managers of the headteachers. This trust central team is likely to include people with headship experience and specialists in areas of corporate leadership. All of them are likely to be as opinionated as headteachers are. Trusts need to pay great attention to the way they communicate not only their ways of working, but also the process by which these are decided on, reviewed, and amended. Getting this right is crucial to all these leaders working together successfully and schools seeing improvements both collectively and individually.

Successful trusts long to see leaders across their schools working together closely and supportively so that all the schools can flourish together. Most school leaders will, in principle, be happy to work in this way. However, when push comes to shove, and pressures mount, each school leader will inevitably be most worried and concerned about their own school. This can inhibit generosity with the resources of each school, particularly its most valuable and expert staff. Trusts have to find ways of working that do not depend on goodwill. Examples of tactics used by trusts include headteachers or other senior leaders having a formal responsibility to work beyond their school, or the formal performance management arrangements for these figures including shared responsibility for the success of the trust not just an individual school.

In schools, as in life, money has the potential to stretch and strain relationships. This is certainly the case in academy trusts. A trust can allocate its overall funding across schools however it thinks fit. Trusts have the freedom to pool their funding, if they wish, and go through specific procedures to consult schools and give the mechanisms to complain about allocations. This is a very significant freedom, but only some trusts are brave enough to take it up. One reason not to take up this opportunity is that when resources are scarce then the trust – rather than the government – becomes the organisation held responsible and criticised for the level of allocations of funds to schools. Overall, however, this opportunity is undoubtedly a tool in the kit of school improvement and not to use it is missing a trick. In all school improvement journeys a key challenge is the capacity of leaders to force the pace and accelerate progress. Choices about how best to use the available financial resources will determine how best capacity is used across the trust.

ASIDE

Benefits of trusts

The following quotes from inspection reports highlight some of the benefits a school can derive from being part of a trust:

'The Trust checks on the school's improvement effectively and provides high-quality support. Leaders at all levels want the very best for all pupils, this is encapsulated by the school vision 'To be the best you can be''

'Leaders have worked closely across the trust to establish an ambitious curriculum that starts in the early years and builds logically to ambitious end points. Well-considered training and a coaching approach are equipping staff to lead subjects well.'

UNLIKELY

Emerging, and indeed experienced, school leaders develop a savviness and become quick at assessing how things are going and how well individuals are performing. This is an essential part of their work and an area in which those aspiring to school leadership need to develop. However, school leaders are well-advised to take care over the judgments they make, for good and bad, and recognise that on occasions they may miss important details. Things you considered unlikely will very likely come to pass. In the busyness of school improvement, be prepared to be surprised!

Busy school leaders will spend a lot of time on getting recruitment right. In really busy times there is a temptation to cut down on the amount of time selection processes take. This is particularly the case when there appears to be an obviously strong candidate against some weak ones. Why spend all those hours away from the other urgent school improvement tasks to go through the motions when it is already clear what the outcome of the recruitment exercise will be? Tempting as this is, it is a mug's game.

There is a risk in an academy trust that some deputy heads get labelled as being unfit to step up to the role of headteacher. This may be result of the assessment of their performance as deputy head, but can also, less fairly, be based on a poor performance in a previous recruitment exercise. It is not right that a single poor interview follows someone around because they are known within the trust while someone from outside is able to come in with a clean slate. If selection panels are determined to be open-minded, they will from time to time be richly rewarded with someone who they thought was unlikely but turned out to be the perfect fit for a post.

Similarly, school leaders need to have the confidence to put themselves forward for promoted posts. It is obviously very nice when someone taps you on the shoulder and suggests that you do so, but if a school leader waits until this happens it may be that they miss out on a post made in heaven. 'You have to be in it to win it'. Putting yourself forward for posts is a tough experience because there's no point applying for a senior post without throwing yourself into it, imagining yourself in the role, and explaining in the selection process how you would expect to go about making it a great success. However, no matter how enthusiastically you portray yourself, it may not be what the section panel is looking for, and you will have to endure the disappointment that follows an unsuccessful application. This can be draining, but for the school leader who wants to take on more responsible posts it is something which they need to be encouraged to go through.

Most people are their own worst critics. All they can see is how unlikely it would be that anyone would want to appoint them to a post even more responsible than the one they already hold. However, there is no one else in the position to make an application on your behalf. School leaders need to seize opportunities that arise and put themselves forward, humbly but with a clear and confident explanation of the skills and energy they would bring to a role.

We all make assumptions and presumptions and bring our expectations to leadership roles. However, these assumptions can undermine key areas of a school's operations and we need to be willing to have an open mind. The country's greatest expert on meeting the challenge of supporting children from disadvantaged backgrounds encourages schools to assess not presume. The same is true with staff. Be prepared to be surprised that the supposedly unlikely can turn out to be the hidden gem. A new school leader will quickly spot the staff they find grumpy and least easy to inspire. A new school leader will do their best not to show how intimidated they may feel by some senior staff. But how exciting for the school leader when staff who at first appeared grumpy or difficult rise to the school improvement challenge. School leaders are much more likely to see this gratifying if unexpected development if they keep any preconceptions and assumptions they have about particular members of staff to themselves. The weaker school leader who has already indulged in gossiping about seemingly awkward colleagues will miss out on an unlikely bonus – and indeed will only have succeeded in further isolating and demotivating those staff.

School leaders overseeing a number of schools will get to know them all very well. When looking across this group of schools, they will form opinions and predictions about the relative rates of progress that each is likely to make in different aspects of their work. Leaders who have risen to this level of responsibility have sufficient experience that these opinions and predictions are likely in many cases to be pretty accurate. Again, however, they should allow themselves to be surprised by unlikely developments that sometimes take place. These unlikely developments can be either positive or negative. However experienced, and however many schools a leader has observed, school improvement still has the potential to delight and frustrate.

One of the joys of a tough school improvement journey is seeing a group of staff that seemed highly unlikely to transform a school come together and change their attitude, skills, and levels of energy. This only happens through exceptional leadership: where the goals of the journey are made clear, the values of the leader are lived not just espoused, and careful thought is given to the collective and individual training and support that staff need. Judging the pace of development is the key. You need to constantly push for improvement but also have an eye to the capacity to take things on. Sometimes a school leader will make a judicious appointment to a position of responsibility of someone who might previously have been seen as part of the 'awkward squad'. Such decisions are of course not without risk, but the brave school leader can reap great benefits with good judgement. Unlikely leaders can emerge when they realise their strengths are being valued and given positive recognition.

For those leading across several schools in an academy trust it will sometimes be appropriate to consider where else in the school system might benefit from their trust's skills and capacity to improve children's education and life chances. Such opportunities will only be a possibility if their own work to date has been successful. The system is still very immature. Although from time to time a trust may be asked by the DfE whether it wishes to be included on a long list for consideration to take on some terrible school they are looking at, it is for trust leaders to take the initiative in reshaping the school system where it is broken. While there are very fine parts of our school system, everyone knows about the terrible bits: schools which have struggled for many years, a special needs system not fit for purpose, and alternative provision that has rays of optimism but in too many places is managed very poorly. Trusts that others may think are unlikely should also seize the day and step forward. This is not easy and will often require free school applications (and the years of effort that this involves).

One trust decided someone needed to do something about the crisis in lack of places for children with severe social, emotional, and mental health needs. It made two free school special school applications, both of which were successful. Five years later, one had opened and had its first inspection – the first time that local authority area had ever had a special school with that designation judged good. The second was only just ready to open. When the applications went in, all this seemed highly unlikely. It is possible.

Another area where surprises occur in school planning is inspections. Trusts with several schools put much thought into estimating the likely terms for each to be inspected. They will look at other local schools and compare when their last inspection was relative to their own. What most trusts learn is that they are very unlikely to estimate correctly every time.

ASIDE

School improvement systems in high-performing countries

Regardless of whether their school improvement systems are based on school inspections or self-evaluation, all the countries considered in this review place a strong emphasis on school-to-school collaboration and peer-to-peer support, although the mechanisms through which this is organised vary.

The school improvement activities instigated by the countries in this review are, for the most part, not time-limited but intended to provide sustainable improvements.

The majority of improvements relate to building the technical skills of teachers and, linked to this, providing increased autonomy for schools to adapt and deliver the curriculum to reflect the needs of the pupils in the school.

Germany and Taiwan, which have achieved high-performing status have used inspection-led systems to identify and support low-performing schools. Most Federal States in Germany use an inspection-led system with low-stakes, with inspection results not generally published and the emphasis of inspection being placed on school quality process criteria rather than outcomes. As a result, schools identified as in need of improvement are often located in socially privileged areas and/or perform well in terms of outcomes.

The way in which countries in this review organise the professional development of teaching staff varies from tightly-controlled processes in Singapore to purely local arrangements in Germany. Estonia and Finland are both instigating more central control of this in response to concerns about variability in teacher quality.

School improvement systems in high performing countries (2019): Department for Education. Available at: https://assets.publishing.service.gov.uk/media/5f22d5f98fa8f57ac683d827/ School_improvement_systems_in_high_performing_countries.pdf

VISITS

I love visiting schools. I have the perfect job because it involves visiting schools all the time! When you visit a school, you see it differently from the way people tell you about it. You see the things that really matter, and the things that nobody tells you. Those responsible for schools need to know them too. They either need to get reliable reports about each school or they need to supplement this by visiting them on a regular basis. Most school visits will be by arrangement, but those who are responsible for schools should also visit more randomly, not to catch people out, but to make clear that schools should be at their best all day every day.

Most school practitioners get only rare opportunities to visit other schools. Schools that are looking for quick tactics to improve the rate of their school improvement journey should consider how to enable more of their staff to get out and visit other schools more regularly.

At an academy trust's annual conference, a group of its staff were asked what ambitions the trust should have for the next three years. The group of staff covered a wide range of roles – senior leaders, teachers, support staff, administrative staff, and staff in the trust central team. Far out on top of their priorities was the request for greater opportunities for collaboration with staff in other schools who do the same role as they do. The trust is considering whether as a matter of course every single member of staff in every single school should be enabled to get out of their school and visit another for at least the equivalent of a school day every year.

If school visits are to be encouraged there needs to be a clear understanding of the benefits. Staff who are told to visit another school and 'sent' on a visit may not have the mindset that will enable them to benefit fully.

How frustrating for a school leader who has gone to the effort of freeing up a member of staff and arranging the necessary cover only to hear a staff member who's been on a school visit say that there was nothing to learn and everything they saw had already been tried in their own school.

There is much that can be gained from a visit to another school, whether that be the feel of a school, specific activities or ways of working that are observed, the way staff interact with each other, the way staff and pupils interact, or the way children relate with one another. Much will be gained from conversations with staff at the visited school, aiding the understanding of why this school goes about things in the way it does. However, the most valuable conversations are likely to be with a colleague where it is possible to make a visit with someone else. Talking about the experience with someone who knows your home set-up gives a rich opportunity for reflection and comparison between the two schools.

One of the most valuable forms of school visit is as a group with a facilitator who prompts and guides both what is observed and discussion about it. Many find the 'Blink' approach developed and advocated by Roy Blatchford to be an eye opener. Experienced visitors to schools learn techniques that provide deeper understanding – such as talking with children, sitting and watching for a period, and asking lots of questions.

A very gratifying moment in a school improvement journey is when – after many years of visiting other schools to learn how they have tackled problems you are wrestling with – your own school is suggested as an exemplar! How open are you prepared to be? There is a great temptation to want to put on a show. It is hard work being the school that is not very good and is clawing its way to respectability. It is hard to remember that working in a not very good school doesn't mean that leaders are not very good. Indeed, not very good schools need the very best school leaders. However, the key to hosting is that visitors are here for their benefit, not to come and marvel at your achievements, however polite they might be about these when contacting you. What will help visitors most is honesty about the struggles and journey of improvement that the school has been through.

There are several activities that can make best use of the valuable time that is given to making a visit. Two such activities are the reporting of the visit itself and then any impact or follow up that took place as a result. School leaders may have regular slots at staff meetings for colleagues to report on visits and the resulting learning. Trustees or governors may provide a regular opportunity for their senior leaders to reflect on the learning they have gained from looking externally and comparing their practice to those elsewhere.

Where visits are more substantial – perhaps even involving travel abroad – the costs involved demand suitable discipline about the formal reporting of what has been gained and learnt. As well as specifics that are gained from visits, in some cases longer-term relationships can be built. These can in turn lead not just to sharing practices but finding co-travellers on school improvement journeys that can be companions across more than just one such journey.

Some visits have very specific purposes. Two examples are moderation and joint planning. Moderation is the technical word used for comparing the work children do in different schools based on similar tasks and curriculum input. The differences can be staggering and, at best, can raise expectations significantly about what is possible. Looking at children's work gets to the heart of how classrooms actually operate – even the presentation of their work says much about the tone set by teachers and what children know is expected. Where schools use the same curriculum, book study gets at whether children have been challenged by what they have been taught or simply spoon-fed information.

Joint planning with staff at another school is immensely useful for small schools, for example in those where staff are the only one in their role (i.e. single staff departments in secondary or primary schools with less than two classes per year group). Planning together is not straightforward and requires quite a bit of time. If schools are serious about supporting such efforts, it is important to understand that they are only sustainable if PPA time is timetabled at the same time for staff in each school. In days gone by, this time would have been used to meet to plan together – now, of course, the travel time can be eliminated by staff meeting virtually.

ASIDE

Visiting schools

Everyone will have their favourite moments from school visits. These highlights might include:

- Story reading in costume.
- Seeing children helped to explain something complex in a way that can be heard and understood by classmates as well as the teacher.
- Displays of work at children's height so they can enjoy their own and their friends' work.
- Lessons that fizz – where a teacher is determined to push children's learning to its limits.
- Children explaining what they are learning.
- Children who are able to go back over their books and explain the progress in their learning.
- Children engrossed in their reading.
- Silence in classrooms where individual work is expected.
- Singing the school song as children prepare to move from lining up at the end of a break to go back to classrooms.
- Observing responses to poor behaviour, and in particular the threshold for needing to call for senior staff.
- Not wanting to leave a classroom because the lesson is so interesting.
- Seeing aspects of the creative and performing arts curriculum that risk being gender-stereotyped successfully avoiding this risk.
- In schools which choose to have allocated children to greet other children, seeing that these include the seemingly least likely.
- Being button-holed to be told how one should personally make changes.
- Seeing the head engaging parents at the gate.

- Noticing changes from a previous visit.
- Albums of photographs in the reception area with highlights of school life.
- The separation of staff room space from space for staff to work.
- Signage that helps a visitor, e.g. 'Visitors are welcome to park here'.
- Seeing a school that is there for the children not the needs of staff.

WALK

... AROUND THE PLAYGROUND

To improve a school requires the right team of people. Getting the right people on the bus is one of the key tasks of a school leader. There is no such thing as the perfect team, but the more dire the situation in a school, and the more rapid the school improvement journey required, the more essential it is to have a team who can work and go together at full pace. However poor a school leader's initial assessments of a staff team may be, it is rare for there not to be some staff able to step up once given the right kind of support. Identifying these people is an important early part of the school improvement journey.

Recruitment to schools doing poorly is not easy and in some parts of the country extremely difficult. Few school leaders have the opportunity to just ditch one group of staff and appoint a brand new one. In most cases school leaders will need to work with the staff at a school and transform them from looking pretty poor to utterly amazing. Where there is the opportunity to recruit, selection needs to be done very carefully. Not only must new staff have skills and experience that will enable them to be key to accelerating progress but they will need to be great members of the emerging school improvement team on a personal level.

Getting the right people on the bus and making sure they are all sitting in the right seats involves making decisions about people. Making decisions about people risks looking for people with the same style and outlook as the school leader. Performance needs to trump style, and competence should trump likeability. School leaders need to be wary of trusting entirely on first impressions – important as these are – and take time to ensure they don't miss staff, who do not impress at a first meeting, but who turn out to be real gems. In particular, there will be staff who will need some support before their true and full potential begins to be seen.

A key skill for school leaders is the ability to have straightforward but difficult conversations about an individual's performance. Such conversations need to be very clear so there can be no doubt about the expectations of staff in their various different roles. Where these expectations are not met, school leaders need to be consistent in the use they make of performance plans and capability procedures. This is not an easy area of school leadership, and one that too many school leaders duck out of. However difficult these conversations, school leaders owe it to their staff and colleagues to be clear, both about expectations and about the consequences of not living up to the jobs that people have taken on. School leaders serious about developing their skills in this area will rehearse conversations with people they trust and take feedback on how to ensure messages are both crystal clear and humane.

One of the most difficult parts of any school leader's job is telling people that they are not up to the job to which they have been appointed. Developing the skills to do this with humanity – without exposing the organisation to any allegation of unfair, unreasonable, or discriminatory practices, and doing so only when it's absolutely necessary – is one of the very important but also less pleasant skills that the school leader needs to develop. Once such conversations have taken place, difficult though they may have been, there will at least be clarity for both the member of staff in question and their line manager.

This chapter is about when you reach the stage when difficult conversations with an individual have taken place – indeed several conversations have taken place – but, the bottom line is that nothing is changing in their performance. The temptation for school leaders is to let sleeping dogs lie. This is to collude with poor performance. School leaders that do not seize the horns with both hands but instead look to find other ways round the issue will end up trying to compensate for the member of staff in question. However understandable this may be, it will be clear to other staff that when you set expectations you are only hoping for compliance. No one rushes to bite the bullet in these situations, but everyone knows when action is needed. School leaders used to say it's extremely difficult to move on staff who are not up to their job – experience is now clear that this is not the case. Rather, the problem is that there are only so many school leaders who are prepared to take on this professionally and emotionally difficult task.

Once it is clear that your task is to tell someone that they are not doing their job and that this is damaging children's education, then it is essential to prepare carefully for this conversation. Even experienced school leaders will check out the specifics of what they are going to say with an HR expert and will carefully compose and write down the key initial sentences. In most cases, there isn't actually much of a conversation to be had. The news should not be a surprise. If it is a surprise, then the preceding conversations where this possibility should have been discussed have not been sufficiently thorough.

The decision to have this conversation will be based on the judgement that without it children are being let down in their education. It does not mean that the colleague with whom the conversation is needed is a bad person, nor even necessarily a fundamentally poor performer. It means that this person is not able to do the job that is needed. (The conversation would often be easier if they were not a decent person who is trying to do well.) The person with whom this conversation is about to take place should be prepared for it and supported through both it and coping with its implications.

In most cases we are talking about members of staff who have, up to this point, had successful careers but have unfortunately ended up in a role for which they are either unsuitable, or have made such big errors that their position is untenable. It does not necessarily mean that they are not suited to school leader roles, but it will mean a setback in their career, and they are likely to need some support in getting back to some meaningful role. The school leaders who take this setback best are often those prepared, hopefully just for a short while, to take a post one stage back from where they had reached.

School leaders need to develop and earn effective relationships with trade unions. This is important. When a school leader gets to the point that conversations have reached the end of the line about an individual's performance, if that leader has earned the trust of trade union officials, then those officials will have confidence that all reasonable steps have been taken. They can then focus on supporting their member in coming to terms with the situation and negotiate hard on a suitable settlement agreement. Some members of staff find this situation so hard that conversations about settlement agreements become very difficult. To have a supportive trade union official fight their corner – rationally and without emotion – can help both the member of staff and their soon to be former employer reach a helpful or at least fair conclusion.

You may have been wondering about the title of this chapter. The euphemism of the 'walk round the playground' comes from a time when heads had only occasional contact with anyone outside the school responsible for oversight of their performance. If the head's position was no longer tenable then the person responsible for the school's oversight would suggest that they take a 'walk around the playground' to ensure there was no risk that the conversation would be overheard and so that the two people involved did not have to have the intensity of looking at each other. Hopefully the system now is more professional and humane.

ASIDE

New headteachers

'When starting out in the role, many heads adopt an open-door policy. At the drop of a hat, they'll attend to any request made of them from parents, staff and children. While such an approach is good for building relationships, there is a risk of headteachers losing control of their own emotional needs and work priorities. You need structure and boundaries.'

Viv Grant

X-FACTOR

There are some astonishingly successful school leaders but by definition not everyone can be exceptional. We all want to improve schools, even us ordinary folk, but although we can all develop professionally we may never be high profile school leaders that become well-known because of our success. From time to time we are fortunate enough to work with people who just have an X-factor that makes their work particularly special. We all look for that magic ingredient.

No matter how self-deprecating school leaders may be none would have reached their positions without already having considerable skills. School leaders in their early years of leadership can feel very green in comparison to their own substantial experience and skills in the classroom. At such times, remembering their own professional development journey to this point should encourage them that they are people capable of rapid skill development.

Hopefully most school leaders have had the experience of mentoring or training new teachers and putting into words classroom management practices which had become intuitive. This experience can help in navigating early leadership and its many new challenges. Articulating problems and taking advice are key to not only navigating challenges successfully but ensuring that each one helps you develop and become a more skilled leader. Through these experiences the thoughtful school leader will reflect on their own responses and dare to recognise that they *can* manage new situations. Some will go further and identify their own personal X-factor: the individual leadership style that they bring to the job that will carry them through both good times and bad.

Let's think through how this looks in practice. A school has a change of head. The departing head briefs the new appointee about the leadership team. They share private criticisms of staff and the sense that they had not achieved what had appeared possible at the start of their tenure. Six months later, not only has the new head settled in, but they are speaking of the senior team in glowing terms. The new head has coaxed a much higher level of performance out of the senior leaders, who are more comfortable in their roles, and attracting much more positive feedback. Each of them has specific leadership characteristics that are shining through and together they have bonded into a cohesive and successful team. How has this been possible? The new leader has set out each leader's responsibilities clearly and coached them in fulfilling the demands of each of their roles. Furthermore, the new leader has identified each individual's X-factor – what they bring to the table – and found ways to draw on and develop these strengths. With acknowledgement of their strengths and scope for personal and professional development, frustrated clashes between members of the senior team have been replaced with an understanding of how to get the best out of each other.

The X-factor is a key element in professional development. Every now and then a new teacher who only looks about twelve years old hits the ground running with such confidence and assurance that a future as a school leader looks highly likely. How tragic when something goes wrong to such an extent that this promising colleague decides to take their skills and dynamism to a different industry. School leaders have a responsibility for all their staff – to foster both their development and wellbeing – but this responsibility is particularly sharp for the potential stars of the future. These stars could take up leadership roles that might impact on thousands of children.

X-factor is just as important for institutions as individuals. One of the head's key tasks is to develop the X-factor of their school – what makes it unique and brilliant – and to communicate it so successfully that the whole school community understand it and are proud to be associated with it. Often school leaders will set this out through a specific set of values that infuse every aspect of the school's work. The most successful generally do not choose too many and work hard to keep the understanding of these core principles fresh for both staff and children.

With the advent of academy trusts, trust leaders have adopted a similar approach, but it is debatable whether there is room for both trust and school values. While a trust's values guide the collective work of their member schools each head and school leader will apply values more successfully if they are specific to their own school. Successful trusts will, however, also expect school leaders to ascribe to the wider trust's values.

There will also be times when the values of a school must shift. This can be through developments that the school welcomes, examples would be when the school has successfully applied to expand or add specific provision (such as nursery or special needs provision), or when it is linked more closely with another school through joint leadership and/or governance arrangements. There may also be developments that the school does not welcome and are beyond its control – such as an announced closure, or a change in age range or size – imposed from outside.

When schools have substantial changes to their whole set up, as in the examples just described, they need remarkable leadership, whether or not these changes were wanted or expected. Children need a well-operating school, and an X-factor that they buy into and are proud of is part of that. School leaders may well find cautious staff slowly coming to terms with what is required a particular challenge during periods of change. No child benefits from going to school with grumpy staff.

ASIDE

Living and learning

This quote from an inspection report shows what is possible:

'This outstanding school is characterised by pupils joyfully singing, 'We are living, we are learning.''

YEARLY

Every school system is different, but in the UK the annual cycle of terms and breaks is very driven by Christmas and Easter. Whatever variations have been tried for term and holiday dates these two fixtures have always remained important, as has the traditional summer break, still needed of course to gather in harvest.

Schools, strong and weak, develop regular patterns of events that take place at their allotted times across the year. A new school leader will be variously delighted, puzzled, and appalled by what has become baked into the traditions of a school.

New school leaders will often find out the hard way about the unwritten, but widely known, and extremely specific details of events that are held each year and have survived previous changes of school leader. While breathing a sigh of relief after thinking they had successfully carried off their role in a particular school event, the leader's bubble will be well and truly burst by a parent who very bluntly regales them at great length about how none of the leader's predecessors missed out key parts of this event, even though they have been coming to the school for the best part of fifteen years with all of their many children.

Few school leaders realise the long-term positive impact they have when they successfully add to the school's traditions. A well-run music festival can have the knock-on effect of maintaining instrumental teaching and a successful choir, even through changes of staff. Introduction of a new residential trip that fits into a well-thought through programme of developing children's independence may turn out to be the part of school life most treasured by cohort after cohort of children. All school leaders will have their default favourite area where they personally add to the school's provision. However, the experienced school leader learns that while they themselves might lead a choir, they need to stimulate as much interest from other members of staff in the running of a football team, the intellectual challenge of a chess club, or the entrepreneurial spirit of charity fundraising.

Few parts of the school calendar rival the excitement of approaching September. When the summer term ends, school leaders take their break. Secondary schools need to be ready for results' weeks but all schools need to set the tone that we start the year prepared and ready. September is surely the most exciting moment. Staff and children have had a break and should be coming back to school fresh. It is the time for each child and young person to move up to the next year group. It is a time for staff to remind them of the opportunities of the age group into which they have moved. It is the time that thinking schools set the agenda, establish the routines, and embed the classroom culture that will be expected every day. Schools that get this right receive a payoff throughout whole of the rest of the year.

Most schools set out expectations in the first days and week of the new autumn term. The most serious schools will go over and over these routines for several weeks and will pay great attention to every single detail. Some schools do this successfully in relation to behaviour outside the classroom, how children come into school at the beginning of the day and after breaks, and some schools push on from this and set out the culture of learning in every classroom.

September is also when children start both primary and secondary school. These are moments that people remember for the rest of their lives. Thoughtful schools recognise the emotional concerns of both children and their families at such crucial times.

School staff can of course start at all kinds of times during the school year. Generally, however, September will be the time of greatest change, when many new staff may join the school. This provides an opportunity for school leaders to reset expectations and ambitions for the year not just with children but also with staff. September is also the time when there is much analysis of the results the school has achieved the previous summer. All schools take stock of their results and are either pleased or disappointed. Where schools differ is in the rigour of their analysis. No school has perfect results, and all schools have areas where further attention is needed and improvements can be made.

Some people get frustrated with the school calendar. Such a long summer break, really? Do the children in our schools still need the time to bring in the harvest? While there are commonly understood term and holiday dates, some academy trusts are leading the way in exploring alternatives. A few have challenged the long summer holiday. Many more have looked at alterations such as breaking up the autumn term with a longer half term break. School leaders thinking of going down this route will need to be brave as their attempts to change the school calendar will likely be met with caution and conservatism. School leaders need to decide how much capital they have built up, and how much of that will be used in bringing in such changes.

The most organised schools have the best developed school calendars that include all staff meetings and training, all visits and residential events, all major school events and the timescales expected of staff for specific administrative tasks, such as report writing. Academy trusts, at their best, need to make sure that the annual trust calendars are put together sufficiently in advance for schools to be able to construct their own calendars. Academy trusts need to have calendars that are enabling for schools rather than restrictive.

ASIDE

Songs and identity

A feature of schools in many other countries is patriotism, demonstrated in regular use of both national anthems and school songs. Schools in the UK should consider how they might use school songs etc. to foster a sense of community and identity.

Z

... AT THE END, IT'S ALL ABOUT THE CHILDREN

There are many motivations for succeeding with school improvement: personal fulfilment and job satisfaction, the possibility of promotion and new further opportunities, higher pay, recognition and praise from others, thanks from parents and a wider community, and the enjoyment of successful teamwork with colleagues. Not all school improvement journeys, though, lead to these outcomes. Indeed, sometimes the journey can be accompanied by many of the opposites of these benefits.

School improvement often involves challenges, criticism (warranted and unwarranted), disappointments, and misunderstandings where school leaders can become disenchanted and demoralised. Yet, every day a head must relentlessly put on their positive face and lead from the front. At such times, school leaders will question their motivation and why they put themselves through such demands. They will see other school leaders who do not face anything like the same level of challenges but who receive recognition or appear to have a healthy work-life balance. Their own work-life balance may at times feel distinctly unbalanced. They may find it hard to relax. Even though they are doing everything they can to succeed, they still worry that 'the powers that be' might decide that they are not doing a good enough job. Why, oh why, do we put ourselves through this?

In the end, we do it because we believe children and young people deserve better. Whoever created the school system with its flaws and difficulties, it certainly wasn't the pupils at our school. School leaders generally enjoy the company of children and young people, and ideally learn to build effective, respectful relationships that make every child feel special and valued. A great antidote when the day is not going well – even if you are frantically busy – is to spend a short while talking with children about their learning. You will feel that bruised spirit inside you lift and come to life again.

Many school leaders are particularly motivated by the challenge of how education can overcome the disadvantages that some children experience, and that cast a shadow over the results they are likely to achieve compared to their more advantaged peers. Sometimes this comes from their own experience; that education enabled them to get to a position they never dreamt possible.

Academy trusts have a mixed reputation with the general public. There is a fairly widespread view that they are simply businesses trying to make money, and often have highly overpaid senior leaders. The perception of high salaries has some merit – some academy chief executives earn more than chief executives of large councils or the head of Ofsted. Trusts, however, although run as businesses, are also charities and do not generate surpluses for an unpaid and voluntary board.

The overwhelming majority of trusts are founded when headteachers take the initiative to bring a group of schools together. Successful groups have grown either through credibility with other local schools or through the DfE asking them to take on schools needing support to improve. In general, trust leaders share the same motivations as school leaders. An additional motivation, though, is also often a deep anger on behalf of children who attend weak schools and whose life chances are significantly diminished. This anger can motivate a trust to spread its wings to do as much good as it can for as many children as possible.

Individual headteachers can also bring about change. School leaders new to the role will realise that they are listened to in a way they have not previously experienced. If the school is not performing as well as it should be they will probably take the opportunity to make their feelings known. However, school leaders early in their careers need to take advice about when 'to throw their toys out of the pram'. Such action generally gets attention but only on a limited number of occasions. Headteachers need to save up the impact that they can have for the most important occasions. There are lots of things wrong in the education system, not all of which even the most senior people in the education system can put right, simply shouting about them may have little effect. School leaders are well-advised to choose their battles. They should be winnable, values-driven, and where the centre of the argument is the best interests of children. The best interests of children are served by school leaders who have effective relationships with leaders in their own and other connected organisations but are hindered when there is any kind of longer-term personal animosity.

Some schools demonstrate their commitment to their children through the Rights Respecting Award. This award is based on:

- Knowledge and understanding of rights.
- The standards that children can expect.
- Empowering children to challenge when these standards are not met.

A focus on children's rights does not replace a commitment to great teaching and children's progress academically. These approaches complement each other as empowering children and improving the standards they expect enhances the learning culture in a school. These different routes to school improvement are not either/or choices if the top priority for school leaders is to achieve the very best for every child across a school.

School leaders will have moments when they agonise over key decisions. These might include changes in organisation such as moving a secondary school from a vertical house system of tutor groups to year groups, or moving around the year groups that class teachers are allocated in a primary school. They might be more radical, such as a special school deciding to take children with needs that are more challenging to meet than the school has experience of to date. These decisions, and many others, may not be universally popular, particularly with experienced staff at a school.

Even more difficult are decisions about the competence of individual staff and consequent management actions that might be necessary. There are many decisions that are hard for school leaders and generally it's good advice not to rush them. However, running a school means making hard decisions, and these *are* the responsibility of the school leader (although hopefully they will be able to access advice and support). At such times, it is essential to focus on what is best for the children in the school and allow that to be the driver.

The terms in which we talk about schools reveal a lot about our priorities. For example, there are a number of terms that can be used to describe pupils. One convention is to refer to *children* in primary schools but *young people* in secondary schools. Another approach is to refer to all ages as *learners* – so aiming to focus on the most important purpose of school. The blander term *pupils* is similar but less direct. In this book, the term *children* has been used to refer to all age groups. Whatever level of maturity has been reached at whatever age, those in schools are served by the state and those who work in schools are there on authority and with the responsibility to ensure progress. Whatever age they are, children in schools are not yet adults and need the security and reassurance that those leading schools will treat them accordingly, however sophisticated and adult-leaning they may be.

One way of demonstrating a commitment to putting children at the heart of the education system is for them to have a role in staff selection. Many organisations ensure that this is the case. However, too often, organisations feel able to simply dismiss the children's selection of the best candidate for a post if it fails to match that of the selection panel.

ASIDE

Children's Rights

The *United Nations Convention on the Rights of the Child* defines what is meant by 'children', as well as their rights, and the responsibilities of governments. All these rights are connected, they are all equally important and they cannot be taken away.

- A child is any person under the age of 18.
- All children have all these rights.

- When adults make decisions, they should think about how their decisions will affect children.
- Governments must do all they can to make sure that every child in their countries can enjoy all the rights in this Convention.
- Governments should let families and communities guide their children.
- Every child has the right to be alive.
- Children must be registered when they are born and given a name which is officially recognized by the government. Children must have a nationality (belong to a country). Whenever possible, children should know their parents and be looked after by them.
- Children have the right to their own identity.
- Children should not be separated from their parents unless they are not being properly looked after.
- If a child lives in a different country than their parents, governments must let the child and parents travel so that they can stay in contact and be together.
- Governments must stop children being taken out of the country when this is against the law.
- Adults should listen and take children seriously.
- Children have the right to share freely with others what they learn, think and feel.
- Children can choose their own thoughts, opinions, and religion.
- Children can join or set up groups or organisations.
- Every child has the right to privacy.
- Children have the right to get information from the internet, radio, television, newspapers, books, and other sources.
- Parents are the main people responsible for bringing up a child.
- Governments must protect children.

- Every child who cannot be looked after by their own family has the right to be looked after properly.
- Children who move from their home country to another country as refugees (because it was not safe for them to stay there) should get help and protection and have the same rights as children born in that country.
- Every child with a disability should enjoy the best possible life in society.
- Children have the right to the best health care possible, clean water to drink, healthy food, and a clean and safe environment to live in.
- Every child who has been placed somewhere away from home – for their care, protection or health – should have their situation checked regularly to see if everything is going well and if this is still the best place for the child to be.
- Governments should provide money or other support to help children from poor families.
- Children have the right to food, clothing, and a safe place to live.
- Every child has the right to an education. Primary education should be free.
- Children's education should help them fully develop their personalities, talents, and abilities. It should teach them to understand their own rights, and to respect other people's rights, cultures, and differences. It should help them to live peacefully and protect the environment.
- Children have the right to use their own language, culture, and religion.
- Every child has the right to rest, relax, play, and to take part in cultural and creative activities.
- Children have the right to be protected from doing work that is dangerous or bad for their education, health, or development. If children work, they have the right to be safe and paid fairly.
- Governments must protect children from taking, making, carrying or selling harmful drugs.
- The government should protect children from sexual exploitation and sexual abuse.

- Children have the right to be protected from all other kinds of exploitation.
- Children who are accused of breaking the law should not be killed, tortured, treated cruelly, put in prison forever, or put in prison with adults.
- Children have the right to be protected during war.
- Children have the right to get help if they have been hurt, neglected, treated badly, or affected by war.
- Children accused of breaking the law have the right to legal help and fair treatment.
- If the laws of a country protect children's rights better than this Convention, then those laws should be used.
- Governments should actively tell children and adults about this convention.

SECTION
TWO

SECTION
TWO

HOW TO APPOINT SUCCESSFULLY

Appointing a team that together will achieve the next stage of a school's improvement journey is a critical task for school leaders. The longer a leader puts up with mediocrity the longer the journey will take and the greater the risk that the improvement will never be achieved. The appointment of the senior team is the most critical aspect of this – finding the best people and juggling roles to fit them all in can work, but a much better approach is to have a team in mind before deciding on individuals to fill those roles and skillsets. All who remember the failure of the England men's football team's 'golden generation' will recall the pain of watching excellent players that never gelled into a successful team.

To get the best team school leaders are looking for the right people to fill the right posts. Discipline in preparing job descriptions, person specifications, and the accompanying packs of information, is an essential part of the process. Successful leaders are characterised by the rigour they apply to every step.

Most schools have tried and tested ways of going about appointments. While there may be some differences in the details of these approaches, the main difference between schools is the rigour of their processes. We all form quick opinions of people and recruitment processes at their worst are just there to help reinforce first impressions. In contrast the various elements of a carefully constructed selection process challenge applicants but also the preconceptions of hiring managers. The thoughtful hiring manager allows the process to shape and develop their thinking.

The most thought and care will go into the most senior posts. Best practice is to set aside two days for a headship appointment, with only some of those attending on the first day invited to return for the second day. This kind of programme allows for:

- A range of activities involving very different skills in which a successful headteacher will need to demonstrate their proficiency.
- A range of people across the school community to be involved and able to offer an opinion about relative strengths and weaknesses of the candidates.
- Time for initially observed strengths to be tempered with observing areas for development.
- Reflection by the panel at the end of the first day on what they would need to see to appoint a candidate.

A crucial part of the selection process is the selection panel working together. Effective selection panels find a consensus about the best most suitable candidate for the post. Ineffective panel members lobby for the candidates with whom they are most impressed. Selection panels need not to be constrained by time to come to a decision. Sometimes it is obvious to everyone who is the preferred candidate but when there are different views around the table, there needs to be time for all the panel members to understand the reasoning of their colleagues. A useful strategy in this conversation can be to accept a panel member's suggestion (even if it is an outlier) and then talk through what might happen if that person were appointed so that the reservations of other panel members can be aired and tested.

Although the selection process described here is very commonplace, it is worth considering how others make senior appointments. The traditional outsourced route is where a recruitment company assists in identifying possible candidates. After an initial longlisting exercise this company carries out first interviews on behalf of their client, before a shortlist of candidates has a second interview with the organisation. This process is used by some prestigious schools and many large academy trusts. Where recruitment agencies are not used this methodology still offers school leaders a possible two-step process that can be useful either when there is a large number of plausible candidates or when there is uncertainty about the 'type' of background that a successful candidate would need to have.

The Government public appointment process offers another possible approach. The interview stage is far briefer. The most senior posts in the country can be appointed after as little as one 45-minute interview and a meeting with a relevant minister. Although this process might sound on the skimpy side to most school leaders the selection process includes a significant gap between the closing date for applications and the date of concluding shortlisting which allows for rigorous consideration of the candidates.

References – i.e. checking that what applicants have set out in their application can be relied on as true – are a key part of 'safer recruitment'. Sometimes they can also assist in decisions about selection but there is considerable variability in the quality of those that are provided. Poor completion of references is sometimes down to unrealistic expectations. This can be exacerbated by the pressure of recruiting close to any of the three national resignation dates each year.

RECRUITING HEADS WHO WILL COPE

How do you know if a promising deputy will step up to being a headteacher and successfully ride the severe stresses and strains of the post?

Asking behavioural interview questions can help identify candidates with the right personal profile. Here are some examples of common questions drawn from a LinkedIn.com blog (https://business.linkedin.com/talent-solutions/resources/interviewing-talent/behavioral-interview-questions-important-soft-skills):

1. Tell me about a time when you were asked to do something you had never done before. How did you react? What did you learn?

   Listen for excitement about tackling new challenges and a willingness to leave their comfort zone, knowing they'll learn something valuable from the experience.

2. Describe a situation in which you embraced a new system, process, technology, or idea at work that was a major departure from the old way of doing things.

   Listen for eagerness to explore new ways of working and ways to improve based on what they learn, if they discovered a better way, and whether they embraced the change.

3. Recall a time when you were assigned a task outside of your job description. How did you handle the situation? What was the outcome?

   Listen for understanding that their job may evolve and willingness to try something new and take the necessary steps to ensure that they were successful.

4. Tell me about the biggest change you've had to deal with? How did you adapt to that change?

    Listen for acceptance that change is inevitable. Strong candidates will also share how they could successfully adapt to new situations and find the support they need.

HOW TO GIVE BAD NEWS

The journey of school improvement never runs smooth. Harold Macmillan's description of what could blow a government off course – 'Events, dear boy' – also applies to education. Events can throw spanners into the machines of even well-oiled and successful schools and have the potential to completely derail those at less advanced stages in their journey. Unforeseen events are not in the calendar or on the plan. Schools with greater maturity will have contingency plans for events that may not be foreseen but are known to occur from time to time. Schools will regularly refresh business continuity plans, e.g. they will know how to evacuate, or lock down their schools in emergencies, and will train their staff to manage these situations should they occur.

School leaders should sadly not be surprised by tragedies that occur for individual staff or pupils – and the school's pastoral support for both needs to be ready to flex when individuals need immediate support. School leaders may well experience the deaths of children during their time in leadership. This might well occur in some special schools of course, but also in large secondary schools and even primary schools. This tests even highly experienced leaders – they suffer grief like everyone else involved but also have to lead the school community through this period. It can feel that the leader is bearing the grief of the entire school community. However immediately leaders are required to break bad news, they are well-advised to practise what they will say with someone else to help get the words and tone as they would wish it to be.

Where there is time, leaders will benefit from talking with other agencies or others involved in the tragedy. Where an event attracts publicity, the media will want the school leader to comment publicly. Again, most school leaders without wide experience of such demands will need to take professional advice on whether to provide a written comment or agree to be interviewed.

Tragedies require significant follow up within a school community – staff will need support and to rehearse how to discuss the event with the pupils with whom they interact, parents will need to know what the school is saying and also suggestions of what support their children might need, and, most importantly, children need age-appropriate support to answer the questions they will have.

There will be events in the school improvement journey that are not tragedies but might feel like it to school leaders. Disappointing inspection reports or test and exam results hit leaders hard. At such times, while of course lessons need to be learnt, the school also needs leaders who can dig them out of these disappointments. Characteristics of leaders unlikely to be able to do this include defensiveness, apportioning blame on circumstances or particular individuals, or trying to downplay the significance of the setbacks.

Inexperienced school leaders may think twice before sharing difficult or disappointing news with their governors or trustees. This is a mistake. At these most difficult of times for school leaders, the discipline of outlining the issues and setting out a proposed response requires the greatest thought and clarity, and the scrutiny and thinking of governors or trustees – who will care as much but be a stage less emotionally involved – can be invaluable.

When the school does badly – perhaps with the publication of a critical report or school results, or something has gone seriously awry – school leaders need to decide whether their usual communication methods are sufficient. Parental meetings about controversial issues can be very challenging for school leaders but when managed well can be crucial in re-establishing support from parents for the school. Critical to such meetings are honesty and authenticity. Parents do not want to see responses that they characterise as 'politicians' answers', and do not really address their questions. Meetings need school leaders to be able to accept criticisms and engage in what will be needed to improve the particular issues being considered.

There will be times when school leaders need to break bad news to children about tragedies in the school community. Generally, school staff are very good at this, as long as they are in control of their own emotions. As teachers will know, they need to be prepared for very blunt questions about life and death and to be ready with authentic but appropriate responses.

EXECUTIVE HEAD JOB DESCRIPTION

The executive headteacher will:

1. Build and enhance a culture where pupils experience a positive and enriching school life.
2. Uphold educational standards in order to prepare pupils from all backgrounds for their next phase of education and life.
3. Ensure a culture of staff professionalism.
4. Encourage high standards of behaviour from pupils, built on rules and routines that are understood by staff and pupils and clearly demonstrated by all adults in school.
5. Use consistent and fair approaches to managing behaviour, in line with the school's behaviour policy.
6. Value the opinions of staff, pupils, and parents while gaining their respect and cooperation.
7. Establish and sustain high-quality teaching across all subjects and phases, based on evidence.
8. Ensure teaching is underpinned by subject expertise.
9. Ensure the teaching of a broad, structured, and coherent curriculum.
10. Establish curriculum leadership, including subject leaders with relevant expertise and access to professional networks and communities.
11. Use valid, reliable, and proportionate approaches to assessing pupils' knowledge and understanding of the curriculum.

12. Ensure the use of evidence-informed approaches to reading so that all pupils are taught to read.

13. Lead the school's response to the challenges of remote learning and enable children to make progress while away from the classroom environment.

14. Promote a culture and practices that enable all pupils to access the curriculum, and have ambitious expectations for all pupils with SEN and disabilities.

15. Make sure that the school works effectively with parents, carers, and professionals to identify additional needs and provide support and adaptation where appropriate.

16. Ensure staff and pupils' safety and welfare through effective approaches to safeguarding, as part of duty of care.

17. Manage staff well with due attention to workload.

18. Ensure rigorous approaches to identifying, managing, and mitigating risk.

19. Manage school finances effectively, including making difficult budget decisions.

20. Ensure staff have access to appropriate, high standard professional development opportunities.

21. Understand and welcome the role of effective governance, including accepting responsibility.

22. Ensure that staff understand their professional responsibilities and are held to account.

23. Ensure the school effectively and efficiently operates within the required regulatory frameworks and meets all statutory duties.

24. Work successfully with other schools and organisations.

25. Maintain working relationships with fellow professionals and colleagues to improve educational outcomes for all pupils.

These specifications are based on *Guidance: Headteachers' standards, Department for Education* (2020). Available at: https://www.gov.uk/government/publications/national-standards-of-excellence-for-headteachers/headteachers-standards-2020.

WORKING WITH TRUSTEES

1. Embrace governance – too many school leaders attempt to manage those who are responsible for governance and then wonder why they don't feel they get much from them. Embracing governance requires expecting to justify each action you make and accepting, and valuing, the conversations that take place around even those decisions that you think are right and you should be empowered to make.

2. Insist that all papers are circulated seven days before a meeting and refuse to add additional papers if they are not ready. Without this discipline, it is difficult, and often unreasonable to expect board members to have read the papers with sufficient care to understand where they should be adding value by questioning specific assumptions.

3. Do not allow those who have written papers to introduce them at meetings. Rather, have them answer questions from those responsible for governance. When questions arise, do not allow answers to include acronyms.

4. There are occasions when trustees have particular skills that school leaders can draw on and find useful. There are times when school leaders are looking for these specific skills. In general, helpful as this can be, it's a bad idea. Trustees are heavily invested in the success of the organisation but their job is to govern and maintain a healthy scepticism about the organisation's own publicity and its enthusiastic leaders.

5. Visiting schools is fun and helpful for trustees in understanding the challenges of school improvement. In general, the leaders trustees have appointed to run the organisation have greater

experience and understanding of schools – that's why they were appointed. Trustees can be excellent without getting to know schools intimately, much as school leaders would like this to be the case.

6. Trustees should be visible to school leaders, and, where there is also local governance of schools, trustees should also be visible to local governors. This isn't straightforward – one effective way is to have an annual strategy day involving trustees, heads, and chairs of local governing bodies.

7. Difficult issues can often be predicted, and sufficient time allocated at meetings to allow these to be properly considered and discussed. Where trustees are not in sympathy with particular recommendations, care needs to be taken about the conclusions the meeting agrees. Often at this stage agreeing to defer is preferable to pushing through a contentious decision.

8. There should be times when trustees meet without senior leaders. This can feel very awkward and needs careful handling. However, discussions should take place and then be shared with senior leaders. It sets the tone for the responsibilities trustees hold.

9. Minutes of meetings and tracking agreed actions needs rigorous attention. The clerk needs to work closely with the chair to ensure senior leaders do not judiciously drop tricky items.

10. From time-to-time trustees need advice from people beyond their senior leaders to ensure there is no, even unintended, shared view (i.e. groupthink) that has actually lost touch with reality. Having an experienced external educationalist as an adviser to the board can help, as can occasional, commissioned, external reviews of the trust's work.

STANDARDS COMMITTEE

There are many versions of 'Standards Committees'. Below are some suggestions about standards committees at trust and school level.

TRUST STANDARDS COMMITTEE (/EDUCATION COMMITTEE/ ACADEMIC COMMITTEE)

- The trust board's top priority should be school standards. A committee should add value to trust discussions about educational standards and advise the trust board on key issues to which it needs to pay attention. The committee should not absolve the trust board of responsibility for standards.

- The membership of trust standards committees (and other trust board committees) will include trust board members and be chaired by a trust board member.

- Membership of trust board committees can be very beneficially enhanced by education experts outside the trust. Typically, the best people will be very busy. Those scheduling meetings need to be cognisant of the availability of such external experts.

- The committee should engage with all performance data available. Papers should always have three parts – a full set of information, a clear summary of what it means, and very short bullet points of recommendations. Long papers are a sign of insufficient consideration. Succinct information shows a clarity of thinking.

- The committee should agree agendas covering the year so it can assure itself that it is covering all aspects of standards, crucially including attention to how well different groups are achieving (particularly SEN and disadvantaged pupils).

SCHOOL STANDARDS COMMITTEES

An academy trust will from time to time have concerns about a particular school. One mechanism used is to establish a time-limited group as a Standards Committee.

- To ensure rapid change, fortnightly meetings keep up the pace.
- 60 to 90 minutes should be long enough to focus on the key issues and to check whether progress is taking place.
- The meeting should hold the school's senior leaders accountable for progress, but also those charged with supporting the school.
- The meeting will look at everything that is wrong in the school and should focus on raising standards. School leaders can expect others to be addressing infrastructure (e.g. buildings problems), and others to be taking a lot of the administrative burden (e.g. urgent recruitment issues).
- Most of the work of the committee is in the preparation for its meetings.

WORKING WITH THE DEPARTMENT FOR EDUCATION

- Treat the DfE seriously – its staff make significant decisions about the way schools and trusts operate.
- Respect DfE staff – they talk a different language to school and trust staff but that doesn't mean that they don't value education or understand the importance of their decision-making.
- Share your news – the DfE does get informed of inspection outcomes in due course but in confidence they welcome early information. Trusts will be happy to do this with positive outcomes. Trusts may demur about negative outcomes but transparency and engaging with disappointment gives a better platform for making the case that a school should stay with a trust.
- The DfE works on a different time zone to the rest of the education system so do not surprised by:
  - correspondence during school holidays.
  - very slow responses from the DfE accompanied by expectations of very swift responses from a trust.
- When a trust is in difficulties, for example responding to a termination notice, always seek a meeting as well as engaging in correspondence. No matter how little of what is said in that meeting makes sense, take careful note of what is being requested, and respond to every single detail.
- Invite DfE staff to visit – they are hard-pressed and do not have a lot of discretionary time but will be delighted to visit – through this you will help them to see the difference your trust or school leadership is making, particularly when external indicators look a bit grim.

- Think about offering the DfE the opportunity to second one of their staff to your school or trust – a few such secondments have taken place and have been remarkably successful and useful for both parties.

- Follow the rules. When a 'business case' is required, use the right form, fill in every question, and complete all requests for information to the full.

- Don't stint on your explanation when you choose not to follow the rules. Having five not four board members is seen as critical in the DfE, while few trusts will see this as crucial in the success of school improvement. If they want five, have five … or be prepared to give a thorough explanation.

- When offered a chance to give an opinion, take it. Don't be sceptical – if civil servants collect views, they will have the job to summarise and share the views collected.

OPENING NEW SCHOOLS

The most obvious way to get school improvement right is to create a school that is great from its moment of inception. In recent years academy trusts have been granted the opportunity to open new schools.

There are various ways to apply for the right to be the trust to open a school. These can range from an open invitation to pitch for a new school (and what as a trust you would add to the local mix of existing schools) to responding to a specific need identified by a local authority, to open a school in response to, for example, increased local population.

Some applications go straight to the DfE with decisions about successful applications eventually made by Government ministers. Selection processes in response to needs for new schools identified by local authorities are organised by that authority, followed by a recommendation of a trust to the DfE, where a senior official will have the responsibility to approve or reject this recommendation.

The timescale for opening new schools can vary hugely. The experience of one trust was:

- Approval in 2015 followed by opening a secondary school in 2016.
- Approval in 2017 for opening a primary school, which was then rescinded in 2022, as the local authority changed its mind.
- Approval in 2018 followed by opening a special school in 2020.
- Approval in 2018 followed by opening a special school in 2023.
- Approval in 2020 followed by opening a special school in 2022.
- Approval in 2021 for a primary school that looks like it will open in 2027.

A new school will generally start quite small so one of the challenges is whether the finances of the school can afford to appoint an experienced head. No one should underestimate the challenge presented by a new school where there are no procedures at all in place and everything is being developed from scratch or transplanted from another school in the trust.

Lessons from opening new schools suggest:

- A head needs to be appointed to start two terms before the school opens (so typically in January).
- The new head needs some availability in the preceding term when the formal consultation to open the school takes place – the only person the local people will want to see is the future head.
- An operations manager needs to work closely with the head before the school opens so that the latter is not completely distracted by the inevitable issues there will be with the school building.
- Getting to 'good' at inspection in the school's third year may feel doable at the end of the school's first year but is a million miles away at the end of the first term of the school's second year – new children and new staff need very careful attention in the school's second year.
- The point of having trusts open new schools is to avoid each head of a such a new school having to work out absolutely everything from scratch. Trust membership allows them to draw on the systems and best practices the trust has developed across all its schools – when appointing the head of the new school, a trust needs to ensure that there is a common understanding about this expectation.

The A-Z series focuses on the 'fun and fundamentals' of what's happening in primary, special, and secondary schools today. Each title is written by a leading practitioner, adopting a series approach of reflection, advice, and provocation.

As a group of authors with a strong belief in the power of education to shape and change young people's lives, we hope teachers and leaders in the UK and internationally enjoy what we have to say.

Roy Blatchford, series editor